THE EUROPEAN HISTORY SERIES

SERIES EDITOR

KEITH EUBANK

ARTHUR S. LINK
GENERAL EDITOR FOR HISTORY

NAZI
GERMANY

ALAN F. WILT

IOWA STATE UNIVERSITY

HARLAN DAVIDSON, INC.

ARLINGTON HEIGHTS, ILLINOIS 60004

Library of Congress Cataloging-in-Publication Data

Wilt, Alan F.

  Nazi Germany / Alan F. Wilt.

    p. cm.—(European history series)

  Includes bibliographical references and index.

  ISBN 0–88295–910–7

  1. National socialism—Germany—History. 2. Germany—History—1933–1945.

3. Germany—Politics and government—1933–1945. 4. Hitler, Adolf,

1889–1945. 5. Germany—Social conditions—1933–1945. I. Title. II. Series:

European history series (Arlington Heights, Ill.)

DD256.5.W495   1994

943.086—dc20   93–6281

                                                                              CIP

Cover illustration: Young girls give the Nazi salute at a rally in Coburg, 1934. Courtesy
of the Imperial War Museum, London. Used with permission.

Manufactured in the United States of America

98 97 96 95 94 1 2 3 4 5 BC

FOREWORD

Now more than ever there is a need for books dealing with significant themes in European history, books offering fresh interpretations of events which continue to affect Europe and the world. The end of the Cold War has changed Europe, and to understand the changes, a knowledge of European history is vital. Although there is no shortage of newspaper stories and television reports about politics and life in Europe today, there is a need for interpretation of these developments as well as background information that neither television nor newspapers can provide. At the same time, scholarly interpretations of European history itself are changing.

A guide to understanding Europe begins with knowledge of its history. To understand European history is also to better understand much of the American past because many of America's deepest roots are in Europe. And in these days of increasingly global economic activity, more American men and women journey to Europe for business as well as personal travel. In both respects, knowledge of European history can deepen one's understanding, experience, and effectiveness.

The European History Series introduces readers to the excitement of European history through concise books about the great events, issues, and personalities of Europe's past. Here are accounts of the powerful political and religious movements which shaped European life in the past and which have influenced events in Europe today. Colorful stories of rogues and heroines, tyrants, rebels, fanatics, generals, statesmen, kings, queens, emperors, and ordinary people are contained in these concise studies of major themes and problems in European history.

Each volume in the series examines an issue, event, or era which posed a problem of interpretation for historians. The chosen topics are neither obscure nor narrow. These books are neither historiographical essays, nor substitutes for textbooks, nor monographs with endless numbers of footnotes. Much thought and care have been given to their writing style to avoid academic jargon and overspecialized focus. Authors of the European History Series have been selected not only for their recognized scholarship but also for their ability to write for the general reader. Using primary and secondary sources in their writing, these authors bring alive the great moments in European history rather than simply cram factual material into the pages of their books. The authors combine more in-depth interpretation than is found in the usual survey accounts with synthesis of the finest scholarly works, but, above all, they seek to write absorbing historical narrative.

Each volume contains a bibliographical essay which introduces readers to the most significant works dealing with their subject. These are works that are generally available in American public and college libraries. It is hoped that the bibliographical essays will enable readers to follow their interests in further reading about particular pieces of the fascinating European past described in this series.

Keith Eubank
Series Editor

CONTENTS

PREFACE

Over the years, books on Nazi Germany have continued to pour forth in a seemingly never-ending torrent. Part of the interest stems, no doubt, from the fascination with its demonic leader, Adolf Hitler. But part of its allure can also be attributed to the revolutionary if invidious nature of the Nazi regime itself. Hitler and his followers did not envisage a state in the normal twentieth-century sense of the term, but a radically different society based on race instead of class, a state, which in their view, was destined to spread across Europe and eventually encircle the globe. That the Nazis never attained their goal of an expanded, all-encompassing, racially homogeneous state does not mean that their vision changed during the Third Reich's twelve-year existence. For racism was the one overarching, consistent theme in the otherwise chaotic society over which the National Socialists, or Nazis, held sway between 1933 and 1945. Though complex, it is a story well worth telling.

During the past half century, many excellent works have deepened our understanding of the Nazi regime. Since these books and articles have approached nazism from almost every conceivable angle, the problem of what to include (and exclude) is fraught with difficulties. Nevertheless, a synthesis is emerging among historians. This book will begin with a brief sketch of the Führer himself, his crucial role in shaping the Nazi movement and his rise to power at the end of the ill-fated Weimar Republic. What follows is a discussion of the Third Reich within its political, economic, social, and cultural contexts. This examination focuses on Germany's domestic scene from 1933 to 1945. Though the Third Reich's foreign affairs will be included in this discussion, its emphasis will not be on Nazi foreign and military policies, crucial though they were, except as they relate to domestic developments. It is obvious, however, that the policies the National Socialists pursued inside Germany took on foreign connotations during the last half of the regime, when most of Europe came under Nazi domination.

This volume also considers a number, though certainly not all, of the historiographic controversies that have arisen over the nature of National Socialism. Were Nazi policies a result of Hitler's intentions, or were they driven by events which he and his entourage created but could not control? Why did so many Germans readily accept Hitler and his ideas and continue to adhere to them almost to the end? Was Germany a special case (*Sonderweg*), or could what happened in Germany have occurred elsewhere? Was the National Socialist movement traditional in orientation, or did it possess, though perhaps unintentionally, modernizing tendencies as well? While reading about Hitler's Germany certainly does not connote acceptance, it should help us understand what was, according to Fritz Stern, "the most popular, the most murderous, the most seductive, and the most repressive regime in our century."[1]

I have incurred a number of debts in writing this book. I am especially grateful to my students whose questions and comments over the years have greatly clarified my thinking. I also wish to thank Keith Eubank, general editor of the European History Series, and Donald McKale for their valuable suggestions, and Ronald Smelser and Gerhard Weinberg for their answers to specific questions. Finally, I wish to thank, as always, my wife Maureen for her support and encouragement, and my grown daughters, Karen and Rachel, who are now beginning to understand what their often preoccupied father was actually thinking about.

---

1 Fritz Stern, *Dreams and Delusions: The Drama of German History* (New York, 1987), 119.

1 / HITLER AND THE RISE TO POWER, 1930–1933

Germany emerged from World War I defeated, disconsolate, and distraught. The government that the German people turned to to pick up the pieces was not the monarchy that had ruled Germany for nearly fifty years, but rather a democratic republic made up of political parties that had long been in existence but had never ruled. They were to be the cement of the new Germany, and the system they created in 1919 was called the Weimar Republic.

Despite the turmoil inside Germany at war's end, the new party-based government succeeded in putting down what was truly a revolutionary situation through a combination of compromise and resolution, compromise with traditional societal elements, yet resolution to overcome groups that threatened to pull the state apart. However, though conditions quieted down, they were far from stable, especially since in the summer of 1919 the government had signed the much-detested, Allied-dictated Treaty of Versailles. Weimar leaders had rightly felt they had no other choice, but by 1920, forces opposed to the republic—especially those on the right—were beginning to recover from the shock of Germany's defeat in the war. They demanded that something be done to restore Germany to what they felt was its rightful place in the world. One of the many groups determined to save Germany from what they perceived as a disastrous course was the National Socialist German Workers' party, headed by Adolf Hitler. Although Hitler did not found the party, he and the National Socialist, or Nazi movement soon became synonymous.

HITLER'S CRUCIAL ROLE

Hitler was born in Braunau-am-Inn on the Austrian side of the German border in 1889. His early life had been far from exceptional. His father, Alois, was a minor Austrian official, who in 1885, married Klara Poelzl. Klara bore him six children, but only two, Adolf and his younger sister Paula, survived. In later years a question, brought on by Nazi anti-Semitic decrees, arose as to Alois's parentage. The evidence indicates that Alois's mother was Maria Schicklgruber, but it is not known who his father was. However, there is no reason to believe that Hitler's grandfather was Jewish, as is sometimes alleged.

The Hitler family moved several times before settling in Linz, Austria, in 1895. Young Adolf led a rather carefree life, but he was not a good student. His fortune changed in 1903 when his father died, leaving his mother with a considerable inheritance. When his mother, much to young Adolf's grief, died four years later, he was again left some inheritance, and he left for Vienna to try his hand at painting or to become an architect. He was turned down twice by the Academy of Fine Arts and began living a bohemian-like existence. While residing at a men's hostel, he painted pictures that were sold as postcards and then turned to painting watercolors, which he sold through a Jewish art dealer. He did all right in this line of work and was further helped financially by yet another inheritance from an aunt. His years in Vienna were formative ones, for it was during this time when he developed not only his self-reliance, but also, given the political and social climate in Vienna, his virulent anti-Semitic and pan-German outlooks.

In June 1913, he went to Munich, ostensibly to pursue an art career but in reality to avoid military service in the Austrian army. Ironically, when World War I broke out, he joined a Bavarian army unit and served with distinction as a messenger on the western front, where he earned an Iron Cross, First Class, an honor seldom accorded enlisted men. After the war, which also made a deep impression on him, he returned to his regiment in Munich. In September 1919, he was sent by the army's political section to attend a meeting, to look into the orientation, of a small, right-wing party, the German Workers' party, which had been founded by a machinist named Anton Drexler. Hitler was impressed by what he saw and heard. He soon joined the party as member number fifty-five and at the same time was named to the executive committee with the number seven. He quickly became the major speaker for the party. In February 1920, the party announced a twenty-five point program. It was a combination of nationalist, anti-Semitic, and socialist ideas, and although socialist ideology had been stricken from the party's platform by the late 1920s, nationalism and anti-Semitism remained cardinal features of Nazi thinking to the end.

In April 1920, Hitler left the military to devote himself full-time to the party. During the next year, he replaced Drexler as leader and began to organize the party according to his own dictates. This reorganization continued throughout the decade, despite some difficulties along the way. The most dramatic event was Hitler's attempt in 1923, in the wake of France's occupation of the Ruhr industrial region and run-away inflation inside Germany, to force leaders of the Bavarian state and other rightists to join him in overthrowing the Weimar government in Berlin. On November 8, Hitler broke into and took over a meeting of political rightists at a Munich beer hall. It was a stormy session, but eventually he cajoled the group into accepting his views on the plausibility of a coup d'etat. But any agreement they may have reached did not last, for the next morning, a march that Hitler had organized to increase his support was met and put down by police and elements of the army. Hitler and other Nazis were arrested, and he was sentenced to five years in prison, though with the expectation of early probation. His nine months at Landsberg prison were relatively pleasant, with numerous visitors and few restrictions. He also used the time to dictate the first part of his turgid, but soon-to-be-famous *Mein Kampf* (My Struggle), which he finished in 1926.

Upon his release in December 1924, he started to rebuild the party. Yet the failure of the Beer Hall *Putsch* had taught him several valuable lessons. The next time he attempted to over-throw the state, it would be by legal means, not through a coup d'etat; and he further realized that in order to gain power he needed the support or at least the acquiescence of the conservative German elite as well as the disgruntled middle and lower classes. He kept these lessons well in mind throughout the remaining years of the Weimar Republic.

With the onset of the Great Depression in 1929, his organizational efforts began to pay off. The party had developed into a national movement and had become the leading element of the various *völkish* groups, whose followers believed passionately in the sanctity of the German community and espoused notions of maintaining a national, racial purity and anti-Semitism. Hitler was now ready to move to a new stage: the struggle for control of the German state. He was able to play upon the fears of the citizenry and to combine them with a strident nationalism that appealed to many Germans.

What type of person was Adolf Hitler? His personality is difficult to plumb, for he prided himself in wearing a mask, of not letting others see his true self. He is perhaps best characterized as an aggressive, bright, charismatic, petit bourgeois. There is no doubt that he was aggressive, that he knew what he wanted and was willing to go to any lengths to get it.

He was also very bright. Although he had little formal education, he impressed others with his grasp of issues and his knowledge of specifics. He had a particularly good head for details and enjoyed reciting facts and figures on such things as automobiles and military equipment, much to the astonishment or bewilderment of the persons he was addressing. In fact, he was constantly trying to prove that he was equal or superior to the so-called experts. This desire to dominate, to always be right, was an essential part of his egocentric nature.

Another prominent feature of his personality was his charisma. Although not impressive physically—he stood five feet, nine inches, and weighed barely 150 pounds—his ability as an orator could be spellbinding. He would start a speech slowly, even haltingly, but soon reach a pitch of dramatic frenzy that thrilled, at times even mesmerized, his audience. He was the consummate actor, playing on the crowd's mood and emotions rather than relying on the content of his speeches to have an impact. His flair for the dramatic was heightened by a number of devices—the Hitler salute, carefully staged ceremonies, torchlight parades. He enveloped himself in an aura of grandeur that almost took on a mystical quality.

But there was also an ordinariness about him. He had arisen from the people, did not live ostentatiously, and loved simple things—children, flowers, animals. He had never married (until the last day of his life), for he said that he was married to the German people and their destiny. His dog, Blondi, was not even a purebred. He was, in a sense, the type of person one cannot help but admire, for here was an ordinary man who had risen to the top.

Still, these seemingly desirable qualities masked a truly brutal, vindictive person. One can see this in his attitude toward others. Toward the elite—the nobility, the bankers and industrialists, the military leaders—he was on the surface correct and attentive, hoping to gain their support, but underneath he harbored an intense hatred of their haughty, aristocratic ways: a hatred that surfaced on numerous occasions during which he ranted at and humiliated the upper-class elements in the company of others.

He did have friends with whom he associated over the years, as long as he could dominate them, for he needed flatterers and dedicated followers around him, not forthright, brilliant individuals. At his mountain retreat, the Berghof, in the Bavarian Alps, he and his entourage whiled away the hours, taking walks and having tea at a nearby inn, watching movies, spending evenings in seemingly endless conversation about the current fashions, raising dogs, operettas and their stars, and, of course, his life and development. While these occasions did afford him relaxation, they were far from enlightening and fit well into his pattern of intense activity followed by extreme indolence.

Although reserved toward women, he did enjoy their company and conversation, again only as long as he could dominate them. So far as anyone knows, there were only two women, besides his mother, for whom he ever cared deeply. One was his niece, Geli Raubel. She and her mother had come to live with him in Munich in the 1920s and took over the running of his household. He was fond of Geli and became quite dependent on her, though their relationship seems to have been platonic. One evening in September 1931, they had an argument, and he had left the house. To his horror, when he returned, he found that she had accidentally shot and killed herself. He was filled with remorse—the gun was his—and it took him some time to overcome his grief.

His other close relationship with a woman was with his mistress, Eva Braun. They had first met in the 1920s when she was working as an assistant in the photography studio of his close friend, Heinrich Hoffmann. Hitler eventually had her move in with him, but in a very discreet way. Although willing to be his consort, she stayed in the background and never appeared with him in public. In a weird twist, he "rewarded" her for her stead-fastness by marrying her on the day before they committed suicide together on April 30, 1945. It is also ironic that even though he and Eva had shared their lives out of wedlock, he had a very traditional view of marriage: as long as women were Aryans, they should stay at home and produce healthy babies for the Reich.

His view toward women paralleled his view of children. He reveled in their adulation, but he thought that, if Aryans, their education should emphasize the development of sound bodies and proper attitudes—meaning National Socialist attitudes—rather than intellectual subjects.

He also basked in the adulation of many ordinary people, but he did not reciprocate their feelings. He wanted to use them—for war and for glorification of the Third Reich—to satisfy his own megalomania, not necessarily for the betterment of their own lives. Tragically, despite his deception, many German people believed in Hitler until the end.

As mentioned, Hitler's own distorted views and ideas had come out of his Vienna days and the impression left on him by World War I and Germany's defeat. Though twisted, his views were simple and straightforward: Life is struggle, and within this life-and-death struggle, certain races compete to get to the top. The race that should always be at the top is the culture-bearing Aryan race, while other races, especially the Jewish race, should be at the bottom because of their weak, parasitic nature. To ensure victory for the stronger, superior Aryan race, a war of conquest must be led by the German nation. The living space gained by eliminating inferior races will allow more food to be grown to provide nourishment for the master race, allowing it to further propagate itself and to expunge the inferior elements in its midst. This crude, Social Darwinistic view—based on race and war—was to Hitler what life was all about, and it was the touchstone of his political and economic thinking.

Although uninterested in the day-to-day running of govern-ment, Hitler was vitally interested in the role the state would play in his revived Germany. The loyalty of his subjects was to be focused on the state—and himself—but the state was to oversee the execution of his racist and expansionistic policies. For him to succeed, he needed a strong state, and the state, along with the party, were to be the instruments of his success.

He also needed a strong economy, but it was to be an economy subordinate to the state. The state was to determine the nature of the economy, not the other way around, for only the state could provide the basis for economic development and expansion. Inside the state, economic competition and private property, in accord with his Darwinistic thinking, were to be encouraged, but only in so far as they conformed to the needs of the state. State policy was to be paramount, and the economy was to be its servant.

THE NATIONAL SOCIALIST MOVEMENT

Hitler's ideas also carried over to the party he shaped. At first it centered in Bavaria and was only one of numerous *völkish* groups that had sprung up all over Germany after World War I. While still retaining its Bavarian base, by 1921 the Nazi movement began to expand to cities outside Bavaria, and it also started to develop the structure of a fully organized political party.

One of the new elements was the *Sturmabteilung* or Storm Troopers, more commonly known as the SA. Its main functions were to clear the streets to protect Nazi party rallies from being disrupted, and, at the same time, to break up the meetings of other political parties. As the paramilitary force of the party, the SA recruited many members from free corps bands of ex-soldiers, who had been originally hired by the government after the war to supplement the inadequate regular armed forces but had eventually came under the employ of various rightist groups, including the Nazi party. To give the SA a distinctive appearance, its members—and party leaders—wore uniforms of brown shirts bearing party badges and white armbands with black swastikas printed on them. The swastika was an ancient symbol invoking the power of the sun. Though not unique to Germany, the swastika had been adopted earlier by occult, *völkish* groups in Central Europe to display their anti-Semitic tendencies and thus became attractive to Hitler and his party.

Another addition to the movement was a newspaper. In

December 1920, the National Socialists purchased a little-known weekly, the *Völkischer Beobachter* (People's Observer). Dietrich Eckart, a poet and dramatist who believed deeply in Hitler and who introduced him to some of the leading figures in Munich society, became the paper's first editor and was soon joined by Alfred Rosenberg, later one of National Socialism's foremost theorists, as coeditor. By the time of Eckart's death in 1923, the *Völkischer Beobachter* had become a daily with a circulation of 25,000 copies. Also in 1923, another Nazi, Julius Streicher, started publishing a blatant anti-Semitic weekly, *Der Stürmer* (The Assaulter), and four years later, Joseph Goebbels began another journal, *Der Angriff* (The Attack). All of these publications featured a strident anti-Semitic, pronationalist message, and all of them well demonstrate the Nazi's emphasis on propaganda to get their message across.

After the Beer Hall *Putsch* of 1923 and with Hitler in prison, the party fell into disarray, since Rosenberg was not the type of person who could hold it together. Upon Hitler's release in December 1924, he began to revitalize the movement. It was not an easy task, for many of the local leaders, who in most cases were still elected by party members, zealously attempted to retain their influence. Nevertheless, little by little Hitler was able to reassert his control, in part through his rhetoric, in part because of his truly excellent organizational ability. From Brown House party headquarters in Munich, his influence spread across the country. Party officials had divided the nation into thirty-four *Gaue,* or districts, which roughly corresponded to the federal electoral districts, and Hitler eventually gained the right to appoint each Gau leader. Many of them were "old fighters" who had joined the party during its early days. Closely tied to Hitler as the supreme leader, yet locally powerful within their districts, these corrupt old fighters, along with Hitler, were to become the "heart and soul" of the movement.

Although the party did not flourish between 1926 and 1929—these were relatively good years for the Weimar Republic—its organization continued to expand. Most important was the creation in 1925 of the *Schutzstaffeln* or security units known as the SS. Originally Hitler's bodyguard, they were closer to him in spirit and in action than their SA counterparts, to which they were attached. Garbed in black shirts with distinctive insignia, the SS were rather insignificant until Heinrich Himmler became their leader in 1929, but they eventually displaced the SA as the most fanatical, dedicated, and ruthless element of the Nazi party. Their motto, "thy loyalty is thy honor," was a slogan they took to heart.

Other groups were formed within the party as well. In 1926, Nazi leaders established a Hitler Youth organization, which was followed by a Student League for university students. The party also started to penetrate the professions and set up affiliated associations for lawyers, physicians, teachers, architects, and engineers. Also established was a Combat League for German Culture to attract and unite individuals from the arts. Even women, who did not rank high on the National Socialist list of groups to be courted, were allowed to found a Women's League in October 1931.

In addition, a number of party leaders in the central organization were named to posts which corresponded to a type of shadow cabinet, including departments for foreign policy, press, labor, agriculture, economy, interior, and justice. The significance of these positions and the other organizational additions was that when the Nazis began their drive for full power after 1929, they already possessed the framework to effectively assert themselves and to have an immediate impact on the entire breadth and depth of the German nation.

ACHIEVING POWER

The appointment of Heinrich Brüning as German chancellor on March 30, 1930, ushered in two simultaneous developments: the demise of republican government in Germany and the eventual triumph of nazism. Though the Nazi movement had already been making strides to become a potent political force before Brüning's appointment, the May 1928 national elections showed that the National Socialists received only 800,000 votes, or 2.6 percent of the total, and 12 seats in the lower house, figures which were even lower than they had received four years earlier. But Hitler and the other leaders decided that they could learn from the defeat by broadening their appeal to include farmers and middle-class elements, instead of concentrating primarily on urban workers. The switch in tactics brought results: party membership in 1929 almost doubled to 178,000, and its financial situation improved as well.

That fall, a furor broke out over whether or not the national parliament should ratify the government-negotiated Young Plan. This was a plan whereby the unpopular war reparation payments to the Allies were to be paid on a steady basis. Though scaled-down from the original payments, it still provided that Germany was to make payments through 1988, and parties on the right, headed by Alfred Hugenberg and the Nationalist party, banded together to agitate against its acceptance. Hitler agreed to participate in the anti–Young Plan drive, which called for a national referendum on the issue. Although the referendum to reject the plan failed, Hitler gained in stature, for he was now seen as less radical and more acceptable to additional groups, including the powerful conservative elements of the middle class. Evidence of his increased popularity can be seen in the Thuringian state election of December 1929, in which the Nazi vote percentage jumped from 4.7 to 11.3 percent of the total.

A few months earlier, the stock market crash in the United States had had almost immediate repercussions in Germany, and the coalition government in power had tried to devise measures to cope with it. However, the parties in the coalition had been drawn from a broad spectrum and had such divergent economic views that they could not agree on common policies to combat the depression. The result was a break-up of the coalition and Brüning becoming chancellor.

Brüning, the parliamentary and right-wing leader of the Catholic Center party, had a definite program in mind: deflation. In the short term, this meant putting Germany's governmental finances in order by cutting expenditures and raising taxes so as to arrive at a balanced budget and to deflate any inflationary trends. In the long term, his goal was to find a way to abolish the hated war reparations that had been imposed on Germany. During the spring and early summer of 1930, the government concentrated on finding ways to balance the budget. As for the depression, it would, in Brüning's view, have to follow its normal progression. Once the economy began to revive, the government might be able to step in to help in the recovery process, but the chancellor and his colleagues accepted the conventional wisdom that economic downturns were part of the economic cycle and that governments could do little to alter their course.

Over the summer, Germany's economic conditions continued to deteriorate. Unemployment rose, as did the government's spending to cover the cost. Moreover, the parties in the Reichstag were increasingly at odds with Brüning and his policies. He did not want to depend on the largest parliamentary party, the Social Democrats on the left, for support; and Alfred Hugenberg's conservative Nationalist party on the right began to oppose the measures Brüning proposed. The final straw was on July 16, when the government proposed a balanced budget bill and suffered a defeat in the Reichstag by a vote of 256 to 193.

Brüning's response was ingenious, but in the end fatal to Weimar democracy in Germany. He decided to take advantage of a loophole in the constitution, Article 48, by which the government, through the president, could rule by decree. The aged president and World War I hero, Field Marshall Paul von Hindenburg, no lover of democracy, agreed with his young chancellor, and Brüning dissolved the parliament on July 30 and called for a national election on September 14. In the interim, he continued to rule by decree and even reissued his balanced budget proposal.

Brüning thought that the voters would give him the support he needed and elect a legislature in tune with his thinking. But the election results were far from what he had hoped they would be. His Center party remained about steady with 68 seats and 11.8 percent of the vote, but the party that skyrocketed into prominence was the National Socialists. Their number of seats increased unbelievably from 12 to 107, their percentage from 2.6 to 18.3 and, most phenomenal of all, their vote total from 810,000 to 6,409,600. In a little over two years, the National Socialists had risen from relative electoral obscurity to the second-largest party in the country. Though not as dramatic, the party on the far left, the Communists, also benefitted from voter discontent and picked up 77 seats or 13.1 percent of the vote, a percentage rise of two-and-a-half points. The Social Democrats remained the largest party with 143 seats and 24.5 percent, but that was a 5.3 percent decline from the most recent 1928 election. The other main party on the right besides the Nazis, the Conservatives, suffered an even more severe setback, decreasing to 41 seats and 7.0 percent. This loss was almost half of its 1928 vote. The extreme parties on the left and right were obviously saying—in the case of the Nazis, shouting—things that the electorate wanted to hear.

Nevertheless, following the elections, Hitler remained determined to attain power legally, and he therefore continued to strive to make the party more acceptable to broad segments of society. In particular, the party toned down its anti-Semitic rhetoric and stressed patriotic and antigovernmental themes, although anti-Semitism was still emphasized in districts in which it was deemed politically advantageous to do so. The movement even started to gain acceptance, if not outright support, from more conservative and upper-class elements, and the party experienced improved finances as well as rising membership.

In the meantime, Brüning remained as head of a presidential rather than a parliament-based cabinet, and he forged ahead with his economic program. He cut governmental expenditures in numerous sectors, including wages for civil servants, prices paid for government contracts, even benefits for the unemployed, while raising existing taxes and adding new ones. But unemployment continued its upward spiral, reaching 4.3 million in September 1931, and tax revenues, as a result of declining production, continued to shrink. The imposed austerity program thus deepened the depression instead of curing it, and most social classes suffered. Even so, Brüning was determined to follow through on his unpopular policies.

Another aspect of the financial picture was that the German economy was especially vulnerable to outside influences. Not only reparations, but foreign loans and credits were also important factors, the latter having played a significant role in resurrecting the economy after the ruinous inflation of 1923. Now, with the depression, foreign credits dried up, and the entire world credit system was weakened. This situation, along with increasing numbers of bank failures, made foreign investors uneasy, and the flight of capital from Germany began to accelerate.

The critical condition of the international economy persuaded Chancellor Brüning to wait before attempting to get reparations reduced. On June 20, 1931, U.S. President Herbert Hoover helped alleviate the problem by proposing a one-year moratorium on the payment of all international debts, including reparations. This move helped, but besides foreign financiers, persons with domestic bank accounts were also becoming nervous about the country's financial condition. The result was runs on banks, bank holidays, foreclosures, governmental inability to handle the crisis, and financial chaos. The government was reluctant to increase the money supply because of inflationary fears, and it went ahead with price and wage cuts.

Despite a willingness to guarantee bank deposits, the government's measures did not endear the public to Brüning. He was ruling by emergency decrees, not by legislative acts. Theoretically, parliament could have repealed the decrees, but the parties were too split to solve the issue. In this atmosphere, radical parties on the left and right made substantial electoral gains, while those in the center continued to lose support.

The political situation was in turmoil. Communist groups were brawling with SA brownshirts for control of the streets, and other party paramilitary groups were also very much in evidence. In October 1931, Hugenberg, the Conservative leader, organized a rally of various rightist organizations, including the Nazis, at Bad Harzburg. Even though Hitler was a somewhat reluctant participant, the leaders of the Harzburg Front emerged from the meeting determined to try to unseat the government. Because of his mass appeal, Hitler, not Hugenberg, soon emerged as the dominant figure to carry on the fight.

His dominance on the political right did not mean that funds for the Nazi party automatically followed, and the Nazis were again hard up for money. Hitler therefore set about to curry the favor of big business, and in a speech before the Industrial Club of Düsseldorf in January 1932, he attempted to allay the fears of those present of his leftist tendencies and to portray himself as a friend of the business community. His appearance before this group has been taken as a sign that businessmen now became favorably disposed toward him, but there is little evidence to back up this claim. Although increasingly disenchanted with Brüning, their reception of Hitler's two-and-a-half hour speech was polite, but hardly enthusiastic, especially among the leading industrialists and businessmen in attendance. Just as important, the speech did not lead big businessmen to make large contributions to the party. In fact, it has become clear that at the time, some, but not many, major industrialists gave substantial contributions to the party, and that smaller, local businessmen actually gave considerably more. Moreover, party-generated funds, such as membership dues, "passing the hat" at rallies, and the sale of newspapers, remained more important sources of income than the contributions of big business. A large-scale financial commitment by the business community was not a significant one until after the Nazis attained full power.

Another event that served to bring Hitler further into the limelight than ever before was the presidential elections of March and April 1932. The 85-year-old Hindenburg was reluctant to run for reelection, but he was finally persuaded to do so. His main opposition initially was a Communist, Ernst Thälmann, and a conservative Nationalist, Theodor Düsterberg, who was also second in command of the Nationalists' paramilitary force, the *Stahlhelm* or Steel Helmets. At first, Hitler was hesitant to run for the presidency, not so much because it would be his first venture into electoral politics, but because of Hindenburg's popularity. There was also the problem that Hitler was not even a citizen, but this was overcome when he had the Brunswick state government appoint him a state councillor, which gave him automatic German citizenship. Though he did not expect to win the election, he thought that the Nazis, as the second-largest party and a growing force at state and local levels, should be directly involved. His candidacy infused a spark into the campaign. He traveled, mostly by car, to seemingly every corner of the nation, preaching his message.

Though predictable, the outcome of the March 13 vote was disappointing to the Nazis. President Hindenburg, whose widespread support included even the staunchest backers of the republic, received 49.5 percent of the vote, Hitler only 30.1 percent. Düsterberg's total was 6.8 percent, Thälmann's 13.2 percent.

Since Hindenburg had just missed receiving a majority, a second election was necessary and duly set for April 10.

Düsterberg pulled out of the race, but the other three candidates stayed in. The National Socialists mounted an impressive campaign. Goebbels, who by this time had been placed in charge of the Nazi's propaganda machine, took full advantage of the opportunity to give the party's candidate maximum publicity, and Hitler introduced a new technique, travelling by airplane, to visit forty-six towns within two weeks, to try to sway the public over to his views. But, once again, Hindenburg proved too popular to be unseated. He received 53 percent of the vote to Hitler's 37 percent, and Thälmann trailed badly with around 10 percent. Nevertheless, Hitler's appeal had reached a wide audience, and Brüning, despite campaigning vigorously for Hindenburg, was losing ground.

Hindenburg himself had become disillusioned with his chancellor, but Brüning continued to pursue deflationary policies that alienated the country's industrial and agrarian elite. When Brüning proposed breaking up bankrupt estates of Junkers, the Prussian landowning class, and distributing them among landless farmers, fellow Junker Hindenburg decided a change was in order. His decision was helped along by Brüning's new defense minister, General Kurt von Schleicher, a schemer of the first rank. He recommended to Hindenburg and his close advisers that Franz von Papen, a nobleman and a firm believer in authoritarian rule, was well suited to head a new government. Like Papen, Hindenburg was a monarchist at heart, and he agreed with Schleicher's recommendation. On May 30, 1932, Brüning was dismissed, and Papen appointed in his place.

Subsequent assessments of Brüning and his chancellorship have been justifiably harsh, for his antidemocratic tendencies and his decision to govern by emergency decrees helped spell the end of the Weimar Republic. Yet some of the measures that he strove to achieve—the end of war reparations and equality of Germany's rights in armaments with other countries—came to fruition soon after he left office in 1932. In addition, toward the end, the Brüning government had finally drawn up preliminary plans for jobs creation projects. These schemes, though modest, were a beginning and were instituted later in the year. Most important, during the summer of 1932, the depression showed signs of slowing, even though unemployment continued to rise with over 6 million persons out of work. The problem was that the general improvement in the economy was not evident until after Hitler had taken over in 1933. The Brüning government might not have been worth saving, but the alternatives turned out to be much worse.

Papen, long associated with the Center party, but officially a nonparty chancellor, had no trouble accepting a presidential cabinet as the basis for governing. His methods—and his goals of a strong executive and a weak legislature—were not unlike Brüning's, but at least the latter had attempted to gain support for his policies from the moderate Reichstag parties. Papen had no such intent. He preferred to rule through the conservatives, tied his chancellorship to the coattails of the president, and eschewed any broad-based consensus for running the government.

Papen applied an example of his methods in Prussia. On July 20, 1932, on the pretext of the Socialist government's inability to keep order there, he had a presidential decree issued to place Prussia under federal control, named himself Reich commissioner, and imposed martial law. He then proceeded to purge the Prussian civil service of its left-leaning bureaucrats and to replace them with conservative individuals who were more to his liking. Germany's largest, most powerful state was thus no longer a threat to Papen's cabinet rule.

At the same time, Papen tried to accommodate Hitler. The chancellor had rescinded Brüning's ban on the SA storm-troopers—hence the violence in Prussia—but he had retained it on the Communists' paramilitary organization. He also agreed to Hitler's demand for new federal elections. The July 31 vote propelled the Nazis into political dominance. They polled 13,746,000 votes, more than double their 1930 total. This translated into 37.2 percent of the vote and 230 seats in the Reichstag. The Communists showed further gains, though only slightly, to 89 seats and 14.6 percent. The Weimar parties remained about the same. The Center party was up a fraction to 75 seats and 12.5 percent, the Socialists down considerably more to 133 seats and 21.6 percent. Papen's closest party ally, the Conservatives, also did not fare well, capturing only 37 seats and 5.98 percent. Obviously, the radical parties on the left and right, especially the Nazis, were continuing to benefit from voter discontent.

Who voted for Hitler? A good deal of detailed research by historians and others leads us to conclude that he received support from all elements of German society, though in varying degrees. The middle class was a key ingredient, but blue-collar workers, professionals, and upper-class voters also supported him. He polled more votes among Protestants than Catholics, and more from rural than from urban voters, but he garnered support from both of the main religious denominations as well as from all regions of the country. Even women, at first skeptical, began to support the Nazis by 1932.

Why did they vote for him and the party? Surprisingly, it was not so much the discontented unemployed who backed him as it was those who feared they might be next to lose their jobs. The National Socialists were able to capitalize on this general discontent, and they became a catchall party of protest. Persons who voted for the Nazis represented vastly different backgrounds and outlooks, but they were united in their contempt for the existing political and economic system. Their support for the party was not particularly deep, but it was sufficient for Hitler and his movement to ascend to power.

Papen did not seem overly concerned about the outcome of the July election. He still intended to rule through a presidential cabinet and expected to have the tacit support of the Center and National Socialist parties. He even went so far as to offer Hitler the position of vice-chancellor in the government. Hitler made it clear that he would accept nothing short of full power; therefore, the Nazi leader and the chancellor found themselves jockeying for political position.

When the Reichstag reconvened in September, Papen had almost no parliamentary support, and Hitler pressured the chancellor into dissolving it and calling for new elections on November 6. Despite a frenzied campaign, and with SA violence much in evidence, the result was a tactical setback for the Nazis. They received the largest block of votes, but their 11,737,000 votes were over 2 million less than they had received three months earlier. Their number of seats in the Reichstag also decreased, to 196, and their percentage to 33.1 of the total vote. On the other hand, the Communist total of 100 seats and 16.9 percent, and that of the Nationalists with 52 seats and 8.8 percent, reflected a continuing rise for all parties left and right of the political center. The moderates remained about the same with the Socialists gaining 121 seats and 20.4 percent, and the Center party 70 seats and 11.9 percent, but neither was in a position to contest for power.

With over 5 million Germans unemployed, the political plot thickened even further. Bereft of parliamentary support, Papen wanted to suspend the constitution and to set up a temporary military dictatorship. But General von Schleicher, the arch intriguer, persuaded President Hindenburg that such drastic moves as Papen called for were politically risky and unnecessary, and that if Papen continued in office his policies might well lead to widespread labor unrest and possible civil war. Hindenburg was convinced and forced Papen to resign on November 17, though the latter continued in the political background.

Schleicher next persuaded Hindenburg that he himself could handle the political crisis, and on December 2, the president named Schleicher chancellor. Though no more democratic than Papen, Schleicher planned to gain the support of big business by offering them tax relief, the trade unions by giving them expanded public works, and the Nazis by granting them a share of political power. Although some in the business community responded favorably to the new chancellor's ideas, union representatives did not trust a political general like Schleicher, and his attempt to entice the National socialists into the cabinet also failed.

His ploy to get Nazi participation was aimed at party stalwart, Gregor Strasser. Strasser was no secondary figure. He had organized northern Germany for the Nazis in the mid-1920s, and later served as Gau leader for Lower Bavaria, a Reichstag deputy, and chief of the party's organization department. Schleicher offered him the post of vice-chancellor in the new government, and Strasser, who was well aware of the party's serious financial difficulties brought on by campaign debts, was inclined to accept the offer. But in a confrontation with Hitler on December 8, Strasser backed down, resigned from the party, and exited from the political stage. The Führer would accept nothing short of head of government, not merely Nazi participation in it.

With Schleicher's lack of success in widening his appeal, Papen again entered the scene. He wanted revenge against Schleicher, and he began conniving with Hitler, whom he thought he could control, to form a new government. After a series of secret meetings between Papen and Hitler and the use of a number of intermediaries, they came to a deal. Hitler was to become chancellor of a cabinet composed primarily of conservatives but also having Nazis Hermann Göring and Wilhelm Frick as members, and Papen was to become vice-chancellor. Papen then convinced the still reluctant Hindenburg that the Nazi movement had to be reckoned with, and that Hitler, not Schleicher, should head the government. Despite last minute attempts by Schleicher to retain power, Hindenburg was listening to Papen and other conservatives who were disillusioned with Schleicher, and on January 28, he resigned. On the 30th, President Hindenburg installed a new cabinet of nine conservatives and three Nazis headed by the forty-three-year-old Adolf Hitler. That evening Berlin was the scene of a seven-hour, torchlight parade. As described by a radio announcer, "A procession blazing torches is streaming up the Wilhelmstrasse.... The banners glow blood-red and against a white background bristles the swastikas, symbol of the rising sun! A glorious, inspiring sight!"[1] The Nazis had taken over power.

---

1 As cited in Bernt Engelmann, *In Hitler's Germany: Daily Life in the Third Reich* (New York, 1986), 22.

2 / PARTY AND STATE,

1933 – 1936

THE NAZI REVOLUTION

Upon assuming power, it almost immediately became evident that Hitler intended for the new government to be revolutionary—revolutionary in image and in practice. The elements on the right—most of the cabinet ministers, the army, the agrarian and industrial magnates—supported him, for they thought he would provide the popular following that von Papen and von Schleicher had failed to provide. They also thought that he would stifle the forces on the left, especially the socialist parties and the trade unions, which they felt stood in the way of Germany overcoming its political and economic problems.

Though correct in their assumption that the National Socialists would be no friend of the left, the conservative establishment failed to appreciate several aspects of Hitler and his movement. One mistake was the conservative belief that he intended to base the German state on class distinctions. His outlook, however, was not to be determined by class but would rely more broadly upon the German people, or more especially upon the German race. Nor did they realize that he did not wish to rule through the traditional elite but intended to control the government himself and to use it and the party as the basis for Nazi rule. These were to be the foundations of the Nazi state. Party and state were not to be bound together, for they were to provide separate functions. Nevertheless, the party, assisted by the resources of the state, was to project the image that the new government would bring about a "national revolution," and the nation would be united behind a government determined to end the economic crisis and to lead Germany forward. Once this image, or "myth," was created, opposition to the regime was made to look treasonous, and with this pressure towards conformity, individuals and groups tended to fall into line. Moreover, measures against outgroups, like the Marxists and the Jews, were also designed to help solidify support for the government. These actions and ideas, along with some violence, help explain how the National Socialists established themselves during the first six months of 1933.

The vitality of the Nazi movement became apparent soon after its assumption of power. On February 1, Hitler and his Cabinet of National Recovery dissolved the Reichstag and called for new elections on March 5. During the ensuing five weeks, and with increased financial support from the industrialists, the party and the rapidly growing SA, whose numbers now reached over 500,000, took advantage of the campaign atmosphere to foment acts of violence and to spread their presence throughout the country. On February 4, Hitler followed the precedent of his Weimar predecessors and received from President Hindenburg an emergency decree to limit public gatherings and to restrict freedom of the press under the guise of internal security. Later in the month, Göring, in his capacity as Prussian Minister of the Interior, ordered Prussian police to support patriotic activities and propaganda with every means possible and to suppress subversive organizations with firearms if necessary. He also authorized the employment of SA and SS personnel as auxiliary police.

An event that occurred on February 27 further played into Hitler's hands. A Dutch ex-Communist, Martinus van der Lubbe, was arrested for setting a fire that destroyed the Reichstag building. Although subsequent investigations have revealed that an SA or an SS group may have initiated the blaze, the Nazis immediately placed the blame on the Communist party. The next day, Hitler had Hindenburg issued a Decree for the Protection of the People and State. It suspended all basic civil liberties, declared that the central government could temporarily take over any individual state that would not or could not keep order, and permitted the secret police to arrest any person and to hold him in "protective custody" indefinitely without right of trial or appeal. The immediate result was that a number of Communists were put in jail and the break-up of other parties' rallies intensified. In the long term, not only did the February 28 decree remain in effect for the life of the Third Reich, but it also marked the beginning of the National Socialist police state.

Yet the March 5 election proved to be a disappointment for the Nazis. They drew only 17,177,200 votes, or 43.9 percent, of the total. This percentage, when combined with the 7.9 percent of the Nationalist conservatives, assured a parliamentary majority of 51.8 percent, but it still fell far short of what Hitler had hoped it would be.

The election setback, attributable perhaps to the disenchantment of many Germans with the growing SA violence, did not, however, slow the Nazi momentum to expand their political power. A highly symbolic act took place on March 21, the Day of Potsdam, at the garrison church where the Reichstag was now to hold its sessions. The German chancellor, dressed in formal black attire, shook hands and bowed deferentially to the octogenarian field marshal and president. The brown-shirted SA and black-shirted SS lined up alongside the regular army. The sermon preached by Friedrich Dibelius, the general superintendent of the Prussian Protestant Church, emphasized that the state must carry out its duties against those who would undermine it so that honor and justice and love would again hold sway over the nation. The new and the old were to be reconciled. There were to be no more Weimars, but a new Reich, a Third Reich based on the traditions of the glorious past.

Two days later, the Nazis maneuvered an Enabling Act through the Reichstag. According to its provisions, all legislative powers were delegated to the executive branch for the next four years. What this meant, in effect, was that Chancellor Hitler had the right to issue laws without interference from the Reichstag. It was truly a momentous decision. Since the act represented a change in the constitution, it required a two-thirds majority to pass, and Göring, by excluding the Communist deputies from attending the voting session and by assuring the Center party that Hitler would not abuse his power, was able to reel in 444 votes, or a little more than the necessary two-thirds. Only 94

Socialists registered their opposition, although there were also numerous abstentions. The renewal of the act four years later passed virtually unnoticed.

From this point on, the Nazis' revolution shifted into high gear. Some of the moves the German people actually agreed to themselves. On March 28, for instance, a national Catholic conference of bishops withdrew the Church's earlier opposition to membership in the Nazi party and instructed the faithful to be loyal and obedient to the new regime. Various professional associations, such as those for lawyers and high school teachers, started to work more closely with their National Socialist counterparts, and the physicians soon followed suit.

Other moves were state imposed. A boycott against Jewish-owned shops on April 1 was suspended after several days because of domestic and foreign protests. But on the 7th, in the wake of the boycott, the government set forth a Law for the Restoration of the Professional Civil Service. This act stipulated that "undesirables," meaning Jews and known political opponents, were to be retired from their posts and replaced by more reliable, conservative officials. The dismissals affected high school and university teachers as well as other branches of the civil service, although it did exempt a small number of Jews who had held office at the beginning of World War I, had served on the front, or had fathers or sons killed in combat. Still the "Aryan clause" was a harbinger of things to come, especially when it soon began to exclude Jews from educational positions and a number of the professions.

At the same time, the government decreed several laws that assured national Reich dominance over the states. It took place in two steps. The first law called for the supremacy of state governments while simultaneously calling for the dissolution of the state legislatures. The second created a new state institution, Reich governors, who were to oversee their respective state governments. In most instances, local Nazi party Gau leaders became the Reich governors.

Later in the month, another anti-Semitic measure became law. Entitled the Law Against Overcrowding of German Schools, it restricted Jewish students to a maximum of 5 percent of the total student body at any individual school or university and to 1.5 percent of the national total enrollment. As a consequence, Jews began to set up schools of their own.

In May, Hitler turned against the trade unions. Much to the gratification of union leaders, he had declared the national day of labor, May Day, a paid holiday. But the next day, he had SS and SA stormtroopers occupy union buildings and expropriate their assets. Still he did not have the National Socialist union, the Factory Cell Organization, take over the other unions' functions, in part because the Nazi union was unpopular with rank-and-file workers, in part in deference to the manufacturers. Instead, he relied on two other institutions. He had a German Labor Front established to concentrate on improving conditions and morale for the laborers, and worker-elected Trustees of Labor were to negotiate any wage settlements. The latter were also made responsible to the government's minister of labor.

A similar situation prevailed for farmers. In June, the Minister of Agriculture and German nationalist party leader, Hugenberg, resigned his governmental post, and a Nazi agricultural specialist, Walter Darré, was named in his stead.

German culture was also not immune from Nazi encroachment. On May 10, some German students decided to perform a symbolic act: they would burn books they deemed inappropriate to the German spirit. Nazi groups proceeded to ransack public and private libraries and gathered together these "unsuitable" works. That evening, books of "decadent" Communist, pacifist, and Jewish authors were burned in large bonfires across the country.

Next came the political parties. The Communists had already been declared illegal in March, and between June 22 and July 5, the other parties were liquidated or voluntarily disbanded. First the Social Democrats gave way, then the early coalition partner, the Nationalists, then three smaller parties, and, finally, the Center party in early July. On the 14th, the National Socialists were declared Germany's only political party. Within six months, organized political opposition to the Nazis had come to an end.

Hitler's government had experienced relatively little obstruction during its early months. It had eliminated, replaced, or penetrated a broad range of German political, economic, social, and cultural institutions. It had succeeded in not alienating the military and manufacturing interests, whom it had alternatively bribed and bullied into collaborating with the state. It had also gained popular support by stepping up programs to provide jobs in public works, housing and building construction, and other industries. Despite the 4½ million Germans still out of work in July 1933, people had the impression that the German nation had turned the corner and that Hitler was responsible for the turnaround. In the meantime, the Nazi dictatorship had been put in place.

PRINCIPLES OF NAZISM

By mid-1933, it was also becoming evident that National Socialism stood for a number of principles. These principles became clearer as time went on, but even during the first years in power, the Nazis adhered to certain major tenets, ideas which formed the bedrock of the Third Reich.

One of their tenets was an emphasis on the national community, or *Volksgemeinschaft*. The first part of the word, Volk, has an ambiguity about it, for it means more than a nation or people. It also has the connotation of a privileged people or race, and National Socialism was based on the premise that certain people were privileged, were superior. There was no such thing, in their view, as equality of the races, and the stronger, chosen people should dominate the weaker.

The Nazi concept of the Volk is well stated in *Mein Kampf*, in which Hitler writes, "We all sense that in the distant future humanity must be faced by problems which only a highest race will become master people."[1] He then adds:

> The highest purpose of a folkish state is concern for the preservation of those original racial elements which bestow culture and create the beauty and dignity of a higher humanity. We, as Aryans, can conceive of the state only as the living organism of a nationality which not only assures the preservation of nationality, but by the development of its spiritual and ideal abilities, leads it to the highest freedom.

---

1 Adolf Hitler, *Mein Kampf* (Boston, 1943), 384, 394.

The quotation actually has two notions embedded in it. One is the negative idea, stated more explicitly elsewhere in *Mein Kampf*, that there is a rank ordering of races in which the culture-bearing Aryans are at the top, and the culture-destroying Jews at the bottom. The other idea is more positive, though it also has negative connotations. It is that the concept of Volk alone is insufficient, it requires community, or *Gemeinschaft*, to give it meaning. The unity of the German people, putting the common good before personal good, is necessary if the community is to move forward. Unity of purpose, sacrifice, and diligence will make the nation strong so that it can deal with the challenges of the future. The Volk community is basic to national greatness.

If there is differentiation among nations or races, then there must also be differentiation within the Volk, and this brings us to a second tenet of nazism, the leadership principle, or *Führerprinzip*. According to National Socialist thinking, the best of the Volk get to the top. The Nazis themselves were involved in an internal struggle in which Hitler eventually won out. A man of prophetic self-assurance had become the self-selected leader because he was the best. If he had not been best, he would not have won out, and the circular argument repeats itself.

Other National Socialist leaders might struggle against each other, but not against Hitler. The Führer was loyal to his party followers so long as they were loyal to him. His system of "divide and rule" allowed lesser leaders—and there was to be a hierarchy of leaders throughout National Socialist society—considerable leeway in return for their loyalty to the Führer as the ultimate authority and arbiter. This led to a number of contradictory policies in the political, economic, social and foreign policy spheres of the National Socialist government. The secondary leaders were able to preach many ideas as long as they were loyal to Hitler, thus many of them, while attempting to get a hold of as much power as possible, set up their own bureaucratic empires in the process. The end result has been described as authoritarian anarchy or a polycracy of power. But despite the overlapping jurisdictions and inefficiencies, the state did move ahead and become powerful under Nazi rule.

The Nazi leadership group was actually a relatively unimpressive lot. Göring, who, among other duties, was the designated heir apparent to Hitler, head of the German Air Force, or Luftwaffe, and one of the nation's economic leaders. Göring had been an air ace in World War I and had access to Germany's elite, but he did not have the discipline to keep at his work for any length of time. Goebbels, the influential propaganda minister, was smart, the only intellectual in this antiintellectual movement, but, despite his club foot, he was also vain, opportunistic, and ruthless. Rosenberg, the party's chief ideologist, was an ineffective administrator who nevertheless intruded into almost every aspect of domestic and foreign policy, all the while propounding his own muddled anti-Semitic, racist philosophy. Himmler, the leader of the SS and the police, who was increasingly involved in the economy as well as in racial policy, had some administrative ability but was unbelievably cruel, and, like many of the others, had a passion for luxurious living. So did Robert Ley, the exceedingly ambitious boss of the Labor Front, who was an alcoholic and a corrupt individual as well.

Among the others, Rudolf Hess, one of the old fighters and Hitler's secretary, was an eccentric, who at one point during the war flew to Great Britain with his own peace proposal. The British did not know quite what to make of him, and he sat out the rest of the war in the Tower of London. His successor, Martin Bormann, was coarse, brutal, and vindictive, but a hard worker, who, during the final years, was extremely influential since he controlled access to Hitler. In retrospect, these are not the types of persons around which one builds an effective, responsive system of government.

Most of them, however, had been with Hitler during the so-called years of struggle, and through this personal bond the Führer maintained control within the party. His followers identified themselves enthusiastically with him and his ideas because he epitomized what they wanted. They were also loyal to him because it was a way for ambitious individuals like themselves to get things done, a way for them to express their own ideas.

Outside the party, control was maintained to a large degree by terror. The National Socialists had long been advocates of political terror, and it had been much in evidence during their run-up to power. They were careful to use it less at the time of their initial takeover, since they wanted to put on a respectful, peaceful front. But once they gained power, and having done so by legal means, they used terror liberally to force the nazi-fication of the entire German society. Nevertheless, their use of terror was in evidence even during the first six months of 1933.

Also during the first six months of 1933, the National Socialists instituted a third major tenet of its thinking, the coordination, or *Gleichschaltung*, of German society. The process was very intelligent psychologically, for the Nazis did not attempt solely to do away with the previous loyalties of the people. Their aim was to tear down the old loyalties while replacing them with Nazi loyalties. Therefore, when they eliminated political parties, they left their Nazi party in existence, and the population was induced to join. They eliminated the labor unions but replaced them with National Socialist institutions. They took over the leadership of the university student league but retained the Nazi equivalent for university students. And they penetrated professional associations and the churches, at least on the formal level, without destroying these institutions. This social coordination benefitted the Nazis in a number of ways: it made the people more easily observed and controlled; it broke down old social ties and limited the peoples' opportunities to voice their discontent; and, by giving a Nazi cast to all organizations, it heightened the possibility that their members would look favorably upon the system being created.

The Nazis did not want to move too fast, however, for they understood that creating new loyalties would take time. They further realized that the most difficult elements to control would be the big-business and manufacturing interests and the military, and the support of both was essential to Hitler. His goal was to strengthen the country for war, but he did not want to weaken it in the meantime by moving too fast and alienating the populace.

Therefore he told the military leaders that he needed them, and they became involved in a slow process of nazification in which Hitler seemingly made compromises along the way. The most-often cited example of mutual concessions was the Night of the Long Knives, June 30, 1934, on which Hitler had the leadership of the SA eliminated. The move was designed to benefit both the Führer and the regular military. The army's concern was obvious. By the beginning of 1934, the SA had absorbed the other party paramilitary groups, had taken in a number of working-class recruits, and had grown to some 2½ million unruly troops. The regular army was limited to 100,000 troops, so it greatly feared the SA as a threat to its power.

Hitler's reasoning was not so obvious, but he was concerned that his increasingly numerous brownshirts, and especially their leaders, might some day threaten his dominant position in the party. Although Ernst Röhm and the other SA leaders had no such intention, Hitler had the army provide the SS, who were more fully under his control, with weapons. With these weapons, on the night of June 30 and the next day, the SS purged eighty-five prominent SA members. At the same time, party leaders used the occasion to settle some old scores, and the SS also killed, among others, Gregor Strasser, Kurt von Schleicher and his wife, and several of Papen's close associates, although not Papen himself.

The results of the purge were many and far-reaching. On one level, it illustrated that the domestic violence that the SA themselves had perpetrated had obviously intimidated most Germans to the point that there was now no serious outcry, despite its blatant ruthlessness and illegality, to the purge itself. On another level, Hitler had done away with the potential SA threat within the party. Furthermore, the SS had increased its status not only inside the party, but June 30 also marked the beginning of SS influence seeping into the military, an influence that accelerated during the war. Nevertheless, the army was still grateful. It no longer had to worry about the SA, and, after Hindenburg died in August 1934, it allowed Hitler to become both president and chancellor and swore an oath of loyalty to him rather than to the state. In the end, then, Hitler gained much more from the purge than did the military, over which, by 1938, he had generally gained control.

Hitler also wanted to prepare the economy for war, and once again he followed a very pragmatic course. He realized that he required certain products to pursue the war, and he asked manufacturers if they would provide them. If private concerns were willing to cooperate, as in the setting up of synthetic oil and rubber plants, fine. If not, then the government would step in. For example, to reduce dependence on foreign iron ore, he wanted to use the low-grade ore processed from the Harz mountains in central Germany. When he asked German mining interests if they would invest in such an unprofitable enterprise, they said no. Thus, the government built the Hermann Göring Iron Works, and the public sector started to expand. Yet the state did not take over industries; it only became directly involved if the private sector was unwilling to assume control of one of its desired projects. No single system was superimposed on the economy, and the Nazis utilized the resulting mixed economy to build a powerful military machine. In this regard, they were ultimately successful.

A final main tenet of National Socialist ideology was to use the military machine to gain additional living space, or *Lebensraum*. In Hitler's view, the superior people must find land to support themselves and to expand. The new land was to be taken for its agricultural utility so that it could support a German population directly. He was not interested in Germanizing the people living in these conquered lands; he wanted to acquire the land for Germans. If the indigenous inhabitants wanted to stay, they would have to accept German dominance of the area, and the inferior elements, such as the Jews, would have to be removed.

Hitler's notion precluded the idea of being satisfied with Germany's pre–World War I boundaries. Agrarian expansion meant that restoration to the pre-1914 borders of Germany would not be enough. Germany needed more territory. As he stated in his second book, which was written in 1928 but not published until 1961, "This goal [of restoring the 1914 boundaries] is insufficient from a national standpoint, unsatisfactory from a military point of view, impossible from a folkish standpoint with its eyes on the future, and made from the viewpoint of its consequences."[2] The need was for a war-like foreign policy that would result in Germany getting what it wanted—more land

2 Adolf Hitler, *Hitler's Second Book* (New York, 1961), 144.

for the propagation of the Aryan people. For this there was to be no finite goal. Nazism involved a continuing process in which the acquisition of new land and the proliferation of the population would serve as a base from which to acquire and populate. The process was to continue.

While Hitler knew his overall objective—unlimited expansion—he did not have a specific timetable or mechanism for its achievement. He felt that there might be a war first against France, then against Russia, then perhaps against the United States. But perhaps Russia, because of its agricultural utility, should come first. He was thus willing to be opportunistic about the means of attaining his goals, but the primary consideration was for Germany to become a hammer and not an anvil as it had been in the past.

The intensity with which the Nazis applied their main tenets—a pure race and more space, the leadership principle, and the coordination of society—varied throughout the regime's twelve-year existence, but all of them were ever-present elements as the National Socialists strove to move toward their ultimate goal of a racially based empire.

THE NAZI STATE

On July 6, 1933, Hitler told his Reich governors, "We must now eliminate the remnants of democracy. . . The achievement of outward power must be followed by the inner education of the people."[3] What Hitler was calling for was for National Socialism to move to a new phase—the consolidation of their fledgling authoritarian state.

Nevertheless, the state that the Nazis developed was a curious amalgam. At first neither the party nor the government reigned supreme. The party and the government had their own structures. There was some interpenetration between the two, but they remained separate entities. Even when the party clearly became the dominant force, as it did by late 1936, the government continued to function, so that there grew up between the two a tension that was never completely resolved.

---

3 Quoted in Karl Dietrich Bracher, *The German Dictatorship: The Origins, Structure, and Effects of National Socialism*, 3rd ed. (New York, 1970), 228.

Despite all of the ongoing tensions, Hitler as head of the party and leader of the government did impose a sort of unity. In the governmental sphere, when Hindenburg died in August 1934 and Hitler became both chancellor and president, these two offices were combined into the more appropriate title of Führer. Yet Hitler did not exercise power through the government in the usual way. He met with the cabinet less and less frequently—twenty-two meetings in 1933, nineteen in 1934, only four in 1936. In fact, the cabinet stopped meeting altogether after February 1938. Moreover, no formal votes were taken at the meetings. They were not convened for reconciling conflicting views or for reaching decisions but merely as a sounding board for Hitler. Since the cabinet was no longer a decision-making body, Hitler increasingly made laws by circulating drafts among the responsible departments to settle possible disputes which might arise between them. Having done this, he would then have a law issued.

He made some attempt to keep regular hours for awhile, since his office and Hindenburg's were close to each other. But when the president retired to his estate for health reasons at the end of 1933, Hitler reverted to his old habit of rising at noon, and he went to his office only for special occasions. Most of his work he took care of casually at his apartment, thereby disassociating himself from the normal daily routine of government.

This did not mean that the ministries and bureaus ceased to perform their daily tasks, but it did mean that they lacked the direction one might expect from a smoothly running government. With the legislative and executive functions combined, the civil service was at first more necessary than ever, but by the mid-1930s, party pressures and a lowering of prestige and salaries caused the civil service to deteriorate, despite the fact that almost all civil servants had joined the party. The main problem was that even though many of the ministers and their senior advisers remained in their positions, there began to appear deputies or leaders of completely new institutions, and these individuals were either completely outside or under only nominal ministerial control. Fritz Todt, for instance, the head of the autobahn (national highway) project, was placed under Hitler's

Reich chancellery office rather than under the minister of transport. When the minister of labor took over the Reich Labor Service, which provided personnel for public works projects, a Nazi deputy, Konstantin Hierl, was appointed. Hierl soon pushed the minister, Franz Seldte, aside and established an outside Nazi party Labor Service Association. Though the association formally reverted to ministerial oversight—this time under Nazi Minister of the Interior Frick—Hierl continued to pursue a relatively independent course.

Another example occurred in the Agriculture Ministry. It will be recalled that Walter Darré, the Nazi agricultural expert, had replaced Hugenberg as minister in June 1933, and Darré soon started a Reich Food Estate to oversee agricultural matters down to the local level. Even in this case, however, Darré's control was incomplete, for although Food Estate officials dealt with some concerns of farm laborers, such as wages, Ley's Labor Front handled other matters, such as providing legal advice for farmers. Thus, in the agricultural sector, as in other areas, party and state agencies each exercised only partial control over their jurisdictions.

The same situation applied to the legal system. It was not done away with but augmented and adapted to Nazi thinking. The additions took the form of party courts and SS courts, which dealt with party and SS matters, and special courts and people's courts, which dealt with treason and similar charges. The adaptations to the legal system were less blatant but equally perverse. The Nazis did not believe in an independent judiciary or in rights of the individual, and they did all they could to undermine these aspects of the Western legal tradition. As a result, thousands of Germans were held in custody, never given the right to a trial, and sent to concentration camps or other facilities for short or long periods depending upon which "crimes" they had committed against the state. Surprisingly, most German lawyers did not object. They also went along with the dismissal of Jewish lawyers and law professors and agreed that a generous dose of Nazi ideology should be part of their legal training. They gave the Ministry of Justice authority over admitting lawyers to practice rather than regulating the procedures themselves. Indicative of their attitude was a German Federation of Judges convention at Leipzig in October 1933, at which 10,000 lawyers raised their right arms in the Nazi salute and declared that they would follow the Führer to the end of their days.

At the local level, the Nazi-controlled national government usurped most of the judges' power. In January 1934, one year after the Nazi takeover, Hitler issued a law that abolished the state (*Land*) parliaments—they had already been suspended—and subordinated state governments to the Reich. One year later, the Reich governors in the various states were placed under Minister of the Interior Frick. Also state judicial administration was brought under the national justice ministry, and most of the ministries from Prussia, the largest state, were combined with those of the Reich.

Although many state officials stayed at their posts and resisted nazification to an extent, most regional power accrued to the Gau leaders, many of whom, it will be recalled, had become Reich governors. Because the Reich governors had the immediate right of access to the Führer, they exercised virtually complete authority over their regions. Among the thirty-four Gau leaders were a number of the most infamous Nazis, including Goebbels representing Berlin, Julius Streicher for Franconia, Adolf Wagner for Bavaria, Fritz Sauckel for Thuringia, and Erich Koch for Prussia. During the war, Sauckel and Koch were to gain further notoriety for their acts of savagery against the population of occupied Europe.

Besides the governmental machinery, the party apparatus helped the Nazis expand their reach to every corner of the country. In terms of the party itself, total membership rose from 850,000 in January 1933 to 2½ million in 1935 to a high of 6½ million in 1943. Many of the new recruits were regular white- and blue-collar workers, but many were also from the civil service and the professions. Their participation was highlighted at party rallies. Most parties during the Weimar period had held gatherings to rally the party faithful, and the Nazis were no exception, holding them periodically at Nuremberg during the 1920s. But during the final years before attaining power, the Nazi rallies had been stopped, mainly for financial reasons. After 1933, however, they were revived and attracted an average attendance of nearly half a million annually. Though scuttled in 1939 because of the war, they were propaganda affairs *par excellence,* and one wonders what they would have been like had the Nazis had the added advantage of television, which fortunately they did not.

Propaganda was one of the National Socialist's ultimate techniques, and, in this case, party and state were closely intertwined. Goebbels, of course, had been head of party propaganda for some time, and in March 1933, he became Reich Minister of Popular Enlightenment and Propaganda as well. From these two positions he forged his empire. He had to fend off other Nazis, such as Rosenberg in cultural, Bernhard Rust in educational, and Otto Dietrich in press matters, since they resisted his attempts to move into their spheres. But in the end, he was usually able to take over or to expand into those areas he wished to control.

His view of propaganda was all-encompassing. It was to be the primary means for persuading and indoctrinating all Germans, and it was to permeate every possible communications media— from press and radio to film and the arts. Goebbels's empire was based on a number of principles: make the message simple and continuous; appeal to instincts and emotions instead of the intellect; be selective about the facts one chooses to emphasize; lie when necessary, but only credibly. The message, in the Nazi view, was to have both a positive and a negative content. On the positive side, propaganda was to emphasize the image of the Führer, the importance of the party, the unity of the nation, the strength of the military, the furtive power of the secret police. On the negative side, the apparatus was to stress the vile nature of the state's enemies—the Weimar criminals, Communists, certain foreign nations, Jews, especially Jews, who were accused of everything from starting World War I to precipitating the Great Depression to polluting the Aryan race.

Three examples that demonstrate the diverse nature of Nazi propaganda are their development of the Horst Wessel myth, their increasing control of newspapers, and their takeover of radio broadcasts and promotion of radio listening. Horst Wessel was a former university student and young SA leader who was seriously wounded by Communists in a riot in January 1930. Goebbels used the occasion to issue daily news bulletins from the hospital on Wessel's condition. By the time he died of his wounds in late February, Wessel had become a martyr to the Nazi cause. As a symbol of his dedication, the Horst Wessel marching song was written to raise high the swastika flag in his honor. The song itself became almost a second national anthem to commemorate the Nazi cause.

With regard to newspapers, in January 1933, the National Socialists controlled 121, mainly low-circulation, newspapers out of a total of 4,700. But by the end of 1934, they owned 436, while the total number of newspapers in the country had decreased markedly. In addition, a law of October 1933 allowed the government to control the press and to enforce uniformity. Two months later, the government started its own news agency and placed all former news agencies under it, thereby assuring that even those newspapers not under direct Nazi control would have to acquire their news through the government agency. Through such means, the independence of the press for the most part became a thing of the past.

In radio, by April 1934, the national government had unified all German broadcasting under a Reich Radio company (it had previously been both federal and state), and its director was to approve important broadcasts before they were aired. To promote radio listening, Goebbels had the transmitting power of the stations increased by 30 percent, and he arranged for the manufacture of a uniform, cheap radio called a People's Receiver, or *Volksempfänger*, to be distributed for sale throughout the country. By 1939, 70 percent of all German households had a radio, the highest per capita percentage of any nation in the world at that time. It was thus obvious that Goebbels was reaching an ever-expanding audience with his many schemes, a trend which continued throughout the war, almost until the very end.

Unlike Goebbels's propaganda empire, in which party and state became closely linked, the party also featured a number of separate institutions that were to exist outside the governmental system, but their separation was not always clear-cut. Except for the actual party organization, practically all of the party entities had some relationship with the government, even if it was only nominal. On the other hand, most of the party institutions were not subject to governmental oversight except in the loosest sense. Their primary allegiance was to the party, and they can be categorized into two broad groups. One was divisions within the party, such as the SA, SS, Hitler Youth, and so on, which were integral parts of the party. The other was affiliated organizations, professional and interest groups that became nazified as part of the larger movement.

Among the party divisions, the most important, once the SA declined in significance after the Röhm *Putsch* in June 1934, were the SS, the Hitler Youth, the Labor Front, and the Welfare Agency. The SS truly became an amazing, broad-based organization, some have contended an empire unto itself. As was said, at first it was under SA supervision, but after Himmler assumed its leadership in 1929 it began to differentiate itself from its SA counterparts. Not only did its members wear the distinctive black uniforms, the SS also started to undertake special tasks. While the SA was responsible for security at party meetings and for breaking up those of other parties, the SS was to provide protection for the Führer himself and for other prominent party leaders. It was also to keep track of developments in other parties and to assure the effectiveness of Nazi internal security. The force was entirely at Hitler's disposal and professed unquestioned loyalty and obedience to him. It was truly his elite corps.

Initially its numbers were not large and in fact decreased to only 290 in 1929. But by the end of 1932, it had reached 52,000, and by 1934, 210,000. This figure was still far short of the 2½ million SA stormtroopers just after the Nazi takeover, but, nevertheless, the SS total was considerable, and it was a force upon which the Führer could always depend.

The two main SS leaders were Himmler and Reinhard Heydrich. Both were fascinating if ruthless, immoral, and corrupt individuals. Himmler was the Bavarian son of a Bavarian secondary school teacher. In 1921, he joined the party while a student at a technical institute in Munich and immersed himself in party work during the mid-1920s. During this time he failed as a chicken farmer and took on other jobs. His main concern, however, was the SS, and he became its head in 1929. Once he had assumed this position, he became a dominant force in the party and eventually spread his influence into almost every aspect of the Nazi state. Besides being a master at accumulating power, Himmler was an ideological zealot who believed passionately in Aryan supremacy and in putting down those elements that stood in the way of achieving his perception of a master race. It was he, rather than Hitler, who imposed racial and ancestral requirements for entering the SS, approved prospective brides for SS men, and established special "houses" for the procreation of babies with Aryan characteristics. Himmler developed these racist measures in the hope that they would appeal to his Führer. They did.

Himmler's top lieutenant, Heydrich, was also an intriguer of the first rank, but less ideological than his superior. He was a naval officer of a middle-class background who had been discharged from the navy for having an illicit affair. In 1931, he joined the SA but soon transferred to the SS. He was then named head of the SD, or *Sicherheitsdienst*, the party's security agency. The SD was part of the SS and the party, but not the SA, and Heydrich used his top SD position as a springboard to become one of the most influential persons in the Third Reich. During the war, his anti-Semitism reached a new level when he became one of the architects of the "final solution," or the elimination of the Jewish race.

Heydrich and Himmler epitomize the SS drive for power. Their first, and perhaps most important, step in creating an SS empire was to take over the police system, which they did gradually. The initial move was in April 1933, when Himmler became head of the Bavarian political, or secret, police. He then used the post to make numerous preventive arrests of political enemies and to place some of those he arrested into concentration camps, such as the newly built Dachau camp outside Munich. By April 1934, he had assumed control of all the states' political police forces except for those in Prussia, and on the 20th, Göring turned over his Prussian secret police, known as the Gestapo, to Himmler, though Göring retained nominal control of it. This move, in effect, made Himmler the head of the political police of each state.

Himmler's next and biggest step occurred on June 17, 1936, when Hitler named him to be not only leader of the SS, Reichsführer-SS, but grafted on the additional title of Chief of German Police. As head of the SS, Himmler oversaw the SD's party security operation. As head of the German police, he was to coordinate all police activities, regular or secret, inside Germany. Though officially subordinate to Minister of Interior Frick, in practice Himmler exercised sole authority over the national police throughout the Reich. He reorganized the police into two branches. One branch combined the criminal police and the political police, or Gestapo, into the security police under Heydrich. The other branch, the uniformed or regular police, Himmler placed under another SS leader, Kurt Daluege.

At this point, state and party policies systems further interpenetrated one another. The Nazis seldom replaced the regular civilian police, who continued to fulfill their duties. But many of them eventually joined the party and some of them the SS, and they often helped hunt down so-called enemies of the regime. In terms of security, the state Gestapo and the party SS organizations cooperated with each other and became increasingly indistinguishable. On September 27, 1939, they were amalgamated under a State Security Office, an umbrella organization that still allowed the security institutions a good deal of latitude, and it also made possible the extension of Gestapo and SD cooperation into the occupied areas after the war began. In August 1943, Himmler accomplished the final step of the police takeover when Hitler authorized him to replace Frick as Minister of the Interior.

The SS also took on other functions. One was its assumption of complete oversight of the concentration camps, and in July 1934, an SS leader, Theodor Eicke, the commandant at Dachau, was promoted to become chief inspector of all camps. Another was the development of armed troops. They were never designed to replace the regular army, and their numbers remained small until the outbreak of the war. But during the conflict, more than 900,000 men and women served in the Waffen, or Armed-SS. At first, the Waffen-SS was more fanatically Nazi than were the regular German soldiers, but as the war lengthened, ideological factors became less important and military considerations became paramount. The composition of the Waffen-SS changed as well, for in 1941 Hitler allowed foreign recruits to be taken into its ranks. This move did not dilute SS standards as much as might be expected, for Himmler intended that the SS's ultimate allegiance was not to the nation, but to a supranational racially pure community. Still the racial Germans (Germans born outside the Greater Reich) and foreign troops were seldom integrated and remained for the most part separate from Reich SS formations, even though they eventually comprised more than half the Waffen-SS total.

The list of SS tasks did not end with controlling the police, running the concentration camps, and providing military units. It also undertook an almost unbelievable assortment of other duties. It set up SS special courts to handle infractions among its ranks, thereby underscoring its independence from state and military jurisprudence. It took over or founded agricultural and industrial factories and contracted concentration camp laborers to private enterprises. It engaged in medical, archeological, and academic research. It became involved in the administration of the occupied territories during the war. In other words, its reach seemed to know no bounds. Whether all of the SS's activities would have resulted in a state run by and for the SS is a matter of conjecture, but there is little doubt that the war accelerated the movement in that direction and that Hitler, no longer restrained by regular military or civilian leaders, approved of the SS's increased involvement in all aspects of German society.

Another important party division besides the SS was the Hitler Youth. At the beginning of 1933, it had only 55,000 members, 1 percent of Germany's organized youth, drawn largely from lower middle- and working-class young people, but during 1933 it grew dramatically. In mid-July, Baldur von Schirach, a young and energetic party official, was named youth leader of the nation. By the end of the year, the Hitler Youth had coordinated all youth organizations with the exception of the Catholic groups and had grown to 3½ million young people. It had further become differentiated by sex into separate organizations and by age with groups for 10-to-14 year-olds and others for 14-to-18 year-olds. Some young people joined for fun and companionship, but there were also pressures to join. Teachers were instructed to persuade their students to become members, and eligibility for apprenticeships and jobs became dependent upon having been in the Hitler Youth.

In December 1936, the organization's reach increased even further. It was no longer to be under the Interior Ministry but became an independent agency directly responsible to the Führer. More important, all youth were expected to enroll "voluntarily." In March 1939, the last gap was closed. Membership became compulsory with refusal to join a punishable offense. Still its effectiveness was mixed. It helped indoctrinate youth with the racist and militaristic outlooks that the Nazis desired they have and provided a "training ground" for military service. But since every young person had to join, many joined only nominally and found ways not to take part in its activities. Many were also put off by its growing regimentation and by the ineffective leadership at the lower levels. It became one of those duties that youths were compelled to do, even though their participation was often half-hearted.

In addition to the party's involvement in youth activities, its direct participation in the labor movement took the form of Robert Ley's German Labor Front. It was not established to bargain for better wages or to improve working conditions, but to act as a social agency. Its "Strength through Joy" program gave workers new or updated skills that were considered imperative to spur the military rearmament effort. Its overall objective was to guarantee labor peace and to provide happy and productive workers, and by 1939 it had 22 million members of a total male work force of 25 million. Whether or not workers were truly happy is more difficult to assess. They were employed and they had more inexpensive and different activities, such as organized vacations, available to them than previously. But the workers' standard of living did not improve substantially, if at all, and factory work was still as physically demanding and boring as it had always been. The Labor Front could congratulate itself for helping to keep the number of strikes to a minimum, but worker discontent was never far from the surface. Despite its efforts, the attitudes of the workers toward the government were seldom as positive as the Nazis would have liked.

An often overlooked division of the party organization was its welfare agency. It was exceedingly helpful for the movement, for it demonstrated its concern for the needy while at the same time obtaining funds for relief from sources outside the party. The welfare agency not only assisted the temporarily unemployed and helped support mothers and child care programs, it also organized what was known as Winter Help relief. Every winter from October to March, thousands of agency employees and volunteers went door-to-door and sold badges that were then placed on front doors or windows to show that one had contributed. On days of solidarity, top Nazis and other public figures went into the streets to collect money and thus indicate their concern for the less fortunate. Moreover, once a month during the winter, families ate only one dish, a one-pot meal, for their Sunday dinner. Any money that they saved by not having a regular meal was given over to a block captain later in the day. Despite all of the propaganda, these collections became too regimented, and some people started to resist making donations. Nevertheless, the agency did aid a number of needy people.

One of the party's other important efforts was its coordination of Germany's professional associations. The nazification of these organizations was surprisingly swift, partly because the professional groups voluntarily agreed to a good deal of "self-coordination." It began with loyalty oaths to the government, and by the summer of 1933, most associations went along with the dictates of the state, including the Aryan paragraph, which excluded Jews from participation, and the political principles of the party. Another reason why the professional groups were quick to fall in line was that the Nazi affiliates had formed in the late 1920s and early 1930s for such groups as lawyers, doctors, teachers, and engineers, and they were then used to integrate the larger professional bodies into the Nazi network. By the end of 1933, lawyers, doctors, and elementary school teachers had dissolved their individual affiliates and become part of the National Socialist organizations. Other teacher groups and engineers held out a little longer, but by 1936–37, they too had become nazified.

These associations were willing to purge themselves not only of Jews, but also of "political" undesirables. While those who were purged suffered financially and psychologically, the remaining members were better off, for they now faced less competition in what had been overcrowded fields. Still the "Aryan" professional leftovers did not always adhere to the policies of their associations, and, in fact, many were apolitical and were not even members of a party association. Whether they were members of National Socialist organizations or not, some did struggle to maintain a measure of professionalism and continued to try to perform their best work. Other professionals did succumb to the Nazis' demands, however, as the hideous medical experiments that were conducted at concentration camps well attest, and, overall, professionalism under nazism declined. The expertise, responsibility, and self-government necessary for a profession to function effectively became warped and finally disintegrated under the Nazi system.

Even though the process of nazification was ongoing, by 1936 the system—with its governmental, party, and extraparty components—had become an accepted part of the German scene. The year 1936 also marks a turning point in the history of the Third Reich. By this point the party dominated the state, and although the latter continued to play a role, the party had developed its own bodies that functioned outside governmental control. Big business and industry and the military still exercised autonomy in their spheres, but their interests increasingly coincided with Nazi policies.

The improved economic climate, the called-for rearmament of the armed forces in March 1935, and the remilitarization of the Rhineland a year later, had all proved popular with the rank-and-file German population as well as with the country's elite. The National Socialists were confident enough of their position in the nation to successfully host the 1936 Olympic Games in Berlin in August with a great deal of pageantry. They presented to the world an amiable, reasonable front, and, despite some racial slurs at the Games, many in the world were willing to accept that the Nazis were not as uncooperative and repressive as they had been pictured earlier.

In the meantime, Hitler and his movement had developed a powerful state, a polycratic system, but a powerful state nonetheless. To be sure, it was not tidy. It contained a number of institutions and individuals competing for power side by side, it had benefitted some groups while hurting others, it had made excessive use of police powers, and it had been subject to criticisms for its excesses and high-handedness. Still, it was generally popular.

Yet embedded in its popularity was its darker side—its disdain for the rule of law, its terroristic practices, its expansionistic tendencies, its glorification of militarism and war. These elements were also in evidence by 1936. They had not yet become dominant in the Nazi system, but they were present. The state was not totalitarian—it was too complex and diverse—but it was authoritarian, and after 1936 the authoritarian Nazi state moved to a more radical phase as its terroristic, expansionistic, and militaristic tendencies assumed primacy. It is ironic that in retrospect the period between 1933 and 1936, "revolutionary" though it was, seems rather benign and stable when compared with the years that followed, when the movement became even more radical and gained firmer control over the entire German state. But 1936–39 was also a time during which Hitler and his clique unleashed forces that spawned a world war that was beyond their control and which eventually led to the collapse of the state itself into ruins.

3 / ECONOMIC POLICIES,

1933–1939

OVERCOMING THE DEPRESSION

Although politics—or political decisions—set the tone for the
Nazi state, economics formed an important adjunct. Hitler was
not, as is sometimes alleged, disinterested in economic matters.
He was in fact quite interested, and in this instance, as in others, his solution to Germany's economic problems was a practical one. He wanted to prepare the country for war, but he knew
that he also had to overcome the depression, and to overcome
the depression, he had to enlist the support of the population
and the nation's elite. He therefore attempted to push his long-
range goals of expansion and war, but he also paid a good deal
of attention to his short-range, nonideological goal of getting
the economy moving again.

To accomplish the latter task was not easy. By 1933, the rest
of the world was also mired in the depression, and individual
countries were more interested in saving themselves than in
helping others. In this atmosphere, the nations of the world
turned inward to find solutions to their problems. Germany was
no exception. Hitler realized he needed the assistance of big
business and industry and agriculture and their workers to effect
a turnaround, so, mainly through the government, he undertook a number of measures to stimulate the economy while being
careful not to alienate the people in the process. In this respect,
he was ultimately successful.

The Nazi program for economic recovery was not run according to a comprehensive plan, but included a number of thrusts.
Designed to stimulate demand and expand income, these thrusts
centered around the government, and, to an extent the party,
formulating and carrying out spending and investment policies
in four general areas. First, the government increasingly took

over regulating prices, wages, banking, and all aspects of foreign trade in order to stimulate the economy while holding down inflationary pressures. Second, the government passed measures aimed at stimulating demand indirectly. Taxes, for instance, were reduced for farmers, small businesses, and heavy industry. Though modest, grants were made to newly-weds, to buy household goods and furniture, and to homeowners, to encourage house repairs, and the party chipped in with a small grant to expectant mothers. The government also gave grants to industries to enable them to purchase machines or to hire additional workers.

Third, the state invested directly in industry, construction, and employment. These direct expenditures, when combined with the indirect ones, resulted in a doubling of public investment between 1933 and 1934 and an increase of another 60 percent during 1935. Fourth, and finally, the government also sought to stimulate the private sector by granting contracts and by making concessions to industries that produced goods that the state especially wanted, such as synthetic oil and rubber. Through involvement in these four areas, the government was able to infuse large amounts of capital into the economy. As a result, national income rose, unemployment fell, and Germany started to recover from the depression.

In accord with these general thrusts, the state attacked the economic crisis across a broad front. One of its most pressing concerns was how to finance the recovery. Because of the depression, foreign borrowing was no longer possible, so the government had to depend on domestic means. Therefore the public debt was increased through deficit financing. To find ways to finance the deficit, Hitler turned to a highly respected, economic adviser, Hjalmar Schacht. Schacht had served as president of the Reichsbank, or German treasury, during the Weimar period but had resigned in opposition to the Young Plan. He had then decided to support National Socialism in the years prior to the takeover. In March 1933, Hitler reappointed him head of the Reichsbank, and Schacht managed to provide the means for raising the necessary revenues.

One of Schacht's methods was to channel funds to the government through what was formally a private business enterprise, the Metallurgical Research Corporation, better known by its German acronym as the Mefo Corporation. The owners of Mefo were actually major German industries, such as Krupp and Siemens, but representatives of the Reichsbank and the War Ministry also sat on its board of directors. The government used Mefo as a front organization for awarding contracts to private companies related to the defense industry. The contracted work was paid for by "Mefo bills," which were, in effect, short-term bonds backed by the Mefo Corporation and guaranteed by the Reichsbank. The Mefo bills were then held by the banks, by the Reichsbank, and by private investors and were to be repaid by the government after five years, out of anticipated increases in tax revenues. The government's optimism that the economy would improve was not misplaced, for tax revenues did pick up, and through the banks the government did eventually exchange the Mefo credit bills for ordinary mark currency. In this manner, the government was able to finance rearmament projects on a large scale. Until the end of 1937, it endorsed RM 12 billion worth of Mefo bills. It was also able to keep the scope of the rearmament a secret, which was particularly important during the early years of the Third Reich, when Germany was still subject to the armament limitations imposed by the Versailles treaty. Another aspect of the Mefo enterprise is that it indicated the extent to which the Nazis were willing at this stage to involve industry in helping it "fix" the economy.

For his financial wizardry, Schacht was awarded additional powers and became Minister of Economics in mid-1934 and Plenipotentiary General for the War Economy in May 1935. Schacht, in turn, rewarded his Nazi patrons by pushing rearmament forward, and he further assisted them in overcoming a foreign exchange crisis in 1934, brought on, as it would be later, by a growing demand for imported goods and raw materials, mainly those associated with the rearmament effort. He dealt with the crisis by temporarily forbidding businesses to make interest payments on their foreign debts and by introducing a so-called New Plan, which placed all foreign currency dealings under governmental control. The New Plan was not really new— government supervision of foreign exchange matters had existed for some time—but it did have a new twist. It required importers to obtain governmental permission to engage in foreign currency transactions before, not after, goods were imported. This meant that the government could control the volume of imports and could also ensure that foreign exchange be used primarily for materials it wanted to purchase rather than those desired only by the importers themselves.

Another immediate economic issue that the Nazis faced was unemployment. In January 1933, it stood at some 6 million, but the actual number was probably higher, since the government's figure did not take into account students who had recently left school, seasonal workers, and women in part-time jobs. Yet work-creation programs were rather slow to get underway. A Labor Service program for young people had already been inaugurated by the Weimar regime, but the Hitler government had let it lapse and did not institute one until June 1933, and participation in the program was voluntary. Only two years later did it become mandatory for all males between the ages of eighteen and twenty-five. Those enlisted were to serve for six months, and they performed all types of labor from farm work to public works projects. For women, the Labor Service remained voluntary until 1939, but then it became compulsory for them as well, and their term of service was extended to one year.

Other government initiatives, including contracts for construction and for the manufacturing of armaments, also helped to bring down the number of unemployed to around 4 million by the end of 1933. During 1934, unemployment decreased further to an average of about 2.7 million per month, and in 1935, the monthly average was 2.2 million, or less than 10 percent of the total work force. While this figure may still be too high by present-day standards, it was an impressive achievement when compared with what other industrialized countries had been able to accomplish during the same period. A combination of labor service, government contracts to private industry, and state-funded projects had created sufficient jobs, so that by the end of 1935, Germany was well on the way to solving its unemployment problem.

Another work-creation scheme that was exceedingly popular was the construction of highways, or autobahns. Originally, various private groups and the government had discussed building the autobahns, but no work had begun until after the Nazi takeover. The autobahn project began in September 1933, and though it did not hit its stride for several years, by 1936 it was employing 130,000 persons directly, and another 270,000 indirectly, for such tasks as mixing cement and crushing rocks. Therefore, Fritz Todt's autobahns did create jobs, and their construction helped to revitalize the German auto industry. But whether the autobahns were built with military considerations in mind, as is often contended, is questionable. In fact, they may well have been constructed primarily to link the nation more closely economically and to help promote tourism. Nevertheless, the military was undoubtedly pleased to have a modern highway network at its disposal.

The armed services were also very supportive of another government undertaking—the development of synthetic oil and rubber. The I.G. Farben chemical combine had been involved in developing these products for some years, but they were not yet profitable at the time of the Nazi takeover. Government subventions soon changed their production into a profitable venture, and Farben quickly signed additional marketing and product development agreements with Standard Oil in the United States and Shell Oil in Great Britain, built new factories to produce the synthetics, and set up a new corporation to produce oil from brown coal. These undertakings helped to set in motion Germany's drive for autarky, or economic self-sufficiency, a trend which accelerated later under the Nazi regime.

During the early years, the military benefitted in other ways as well. Hitler made it clear that the peacetime army was to be raised above its 100,000-person limit as soon as possible. Moreover, the navy received increased funds for its expansion, and the air force, though not officially independent until March 1935, started to add planes to its inventory. That same month, Hitler declared that he would no longer abide by the military clauses of the Versailles treaty; that the army be expanded to 36 divisions, or approximately 550,000 soldiers; and that military service be made compulsory for all German males over 18. These moves obviously also helped Germany overcome its unemployment problem and marked the beginning of the transformation of the nation's military into a powerful machine.

Most sectors of the economy fell in line with the Nazis' early initiatives. Big business had reservations about National Socialist plans for greater governmental involvement, deficit spending, and autarkic policies, but their reluctance was overcome by state and party pressures from without and by collaboration from within the firms. Hitler chose to ignore the economic radicals, who pushed for more social measures within his own party, and sought to cooperate with the business establishment instead. As usual, business did not want the state to intervene in economic matters or to limit profits, but it did favor the government's willingness to hold labor in check and to provide political stability. The Nazis, for their part, worked hard during these early years to gain businesses' trust. One example was the naming of Schacht as Reichsbank president. Another was the selection of individual business associations to control branches of the economy, such as banking and energy, and to oversee the economies of regions, such as Bavaria and Saxony. Though officially under the Ministry of Economics, these associations allowed for a measure of "self-regulation" and managed to work well enough to allay business's fears of the regime.

Individual companies went along with the government as well. I.G. Farben at first opposed the Nazis, but then, with financial inducements, such as those they received to produce synthetic oil and rubber, and mounting profits, the chemical giant let itself be drawn into the Nazi net. The automaker Daimler Benz was more receptive from the start. The depression had hurt it severely, and in April 1933 the government gave it and the other car makers a boost by eliminating a high tax on new automobiles, and later, the autobahn program provided a further stimulus for the industry. The government also rewarded Daimler Benz with numerous military contracts, and the automaker built thousands of armored vehicles and heavy trucks for the army and aircraft engines for the Luftwaffe before and during the war. Another struggling industry, coal mining, was also hurt by the depression, and although it recovered, it never had the capital to become as robust as the chemical and auto industries. Still, most big businesses profited from their Nazi connection.

Small businesses were not as fortunate. National Socialist rhetoric extolled their importance and even passed a Law for the Protection of Retail Trade in May 1933 and organized a new association for trading people a month later. But the rhetoric soon gave way to a different type of economy than what small business had visualized. Many were vulnerable to Nazi policies that emphasized rearmament and big projects at the expense of more diverse, traditional items, such as food and textile products. In addition, the government wanted cheap goods, not highly crafted items, and the number of artisans in the country decreased accordingly. And even had small businesses been able to compete, the increases in raw material and labor costs could not be passed on to customers because of price controls. Small businesses did benefit from the confiscation of Jewish businesses, but between 1932 and 1938, gross output for consumer industries still expanded by only 38 percent, while heavy industry increased almost 200 percent. In a climate that stressed military hardware and cartelization, small businesses simply had trouble competing, and thousands failed during the 1930s.

Another segment of the economy that experienced difficulties under the Nazi regime was agriculture. Its situation was similar to that of small business in that it was caught up in the worldwide trend that saw its value diminish in relation to industry. But even more than small business, agriculture was a revered part of the Nazis' blood and soil ideology. From the beginning, the National Socialists promoted agriculture. The cornerstone of their policies was the Reich Food Estate. Although separate yet nominally connected with the government, it was established in September 1933, and it was to regulate production and distribution, fix wages and prices, and take all measures that agricultural minister Darré deemed necessary. It fulfilled a demand of the farmers to ensure stable prices and wages while still allowing them to turn a fair profit. Another of the farmers' demands was realized with the Hereditary Farm Law of May 1933. The law applied to all farms between 18 and 310 acres, those farms large enough to support a family without requiring additional revenues. These farms were not to be sold or mortgaged and were to be bequeathed to a sole male heir, as long as he had a "German" background. As for the undesignated heirs, they were to be given credits to help them develop new farms, though little came of the scheme since the government appropriated almost no funding to support it. The Nazis also encouraged farming by holding a harvest festival each fall at Bückeberg near Hameln and an annual Farm Congress at Goslar, where professional and technical aspects of agriculture were discussed.

All of these farm initiatives met with mixed results. Agricultural output inside Germany rose from providing 68 percent of the nation's food requirements in 1928 to an estimated 80 to 85 percent in 1939, though some products, especially fats, remained in short supply. Moreover, the drift from the land continued. Besides the incentives, the government promulgated several laws in 1934 to prevent experienced farm laborers from moving to other jobs without governmental consent. But life on a farm still translated into hard work, long hours, low wages, and poor living conditions (65 percent of the farms had no running water). Therefore, by 1939 there were 1½ million fewer agricultural laborers than there had been in 1933, and the nation's rural population had declined from 21 to 18 percent of the total.

While the National Socialist regime undertook numerous measures to encourage big business and agriculture, its policies toward factory and farm labor were more equivocal. They wanted labor support, but they also wanted a docile, controllable, and productive work force. With the dissolution of the trade unions, the Nazis came to depend on Councils of Trust, Trustees of Labor, and the German Labor Front, which took the place of trade unions, to carry out their program. The Councils of Trust and the Trustees of Labor were not at this point to negotiate for wages and benefits, since wages had been frozen at their 1933 levels, but they were to foster worker solidarity by promoting efficiency, better working conditions, and peaceful relations with management. However, since the Trustee groups came to be made up of party members and were responsible to the government, their willingness to deal with worker grievances is open to question.

The party's Labor Front, headed by Robert Ley, was more successful and had a considerable impact. It was not a bargaining, but a social agency, and it moved into many areas. Perhaps its most important program was vocational training. By the end of 1936, a Labor Front subsidiary had opened 400 apprenticeship schools with another 150 under construction and had hired 25,000 vocational teachers who had given courses to 2½ million laborers. Ley's organization also promoted a variety of leisure activities for laborers, including recreation, cultural events, and low-cost vacations. While more workers were able to take advantage of nearby holidays than Mediterranean cruises, Ley's so-called "Strength through Joy" program was quite popular. So was "Strength through Joy's" buy a Volkswagen, or People's Car, plan. According to this scheme, begun in 1938, all workers could eventually own a Volkswagen by setting aside a portion of their paychecks each week. The program was never realized, however, because of the outbreak of the war, and the newly created Volkswagen plants were quickly restructured to manufacture military vehicles instead. Less important was the "Beauty of Work" campaign, which was to persuade management to improve working conditions within the factories. Even though many employers might have done so on their own, over the years thousands of work areas were repainted, outside sports facilities were built, and changing rooms and cafeterias were added to many plants. Though it is questionable whether or not many workers actually used the improved facilities, the improvements indicate the Labor Front's concern for the ordinary laborer.

The Labor Front therefore became more of an advocate for the worker than was originally envisaged, and it began to compete with other party and governmental agencies, the business community, and even the military for a say in broader economic matters. Although Labor Front advocacy did not eliminate the normal tensions that exist in employer-employee relations, it did help reduce them.

Nevertheless, benefits for workers were often offset by compulsory measures. At first, employers were able to get around the wage freeze by paying Christmas bonuses and social insurance and other benefits that the employee usually paid, but in 1935, the government instituted work books, which were a record of one's employment, and which one had to present to an employer in order to move to a different job. Though not completely effective, the works books assisted the state in controlling and directing the labor force into areas it considered of high priority. Yet, to the millions of unemployed in 1933, these restrictions on one's freedom of movement and the loss of trade-union representation were less important than being employed and having some opportunity for advancement.

By late 1935–36, Nazi economic policies were bringing increasingly favorable results. In mid-1936, unemployment had been reduced even further, to 1½ million. Big business had revived and felt that it still had a say over its own affairs despite high taxes, limits on profits, and increased governmental "guidance." The military had benefitted since much of the recovery, over 80 percent of governmental investments, had been devoted to rearmament. Agriculture had continued to experience difficulties, but steps had been taken to try to alleviate its problems. Most important, the Nazis were no longer conceived of as a bunch of wild-eyed radicals who could not be trusted. They were bringing Germany out of the depression, establishing a strong state, creating a powerful economic edifice in which the people, or at least the "right" people, could be proud, especially in relation to the rest of the world.

Still, Germany's economic success was causing its own problems. The armaments and public works boom meant an enormous increase in the demand for raw materials and other goods from abroad. But Germany did not have sufficient gold and currency reserves to pay for the imports, so yet another balance-of-payments crisis was in the offing. Schacht advocated that businesses increase exports to get the necessary foreign currency, but export prices were unfavorable because of the protectionist policies then being followed by other countries, and any diversion of supply from the domestic market would slow rearmament. Moreover, German agricultural products, especially fats and meat, had failed to keep pace with the rising demand brought on by increased employment, and the result was a growing pressure to import more food. The crisis intensified in the summer of 1936. Munitions factories were producing at only 70 percent of capacity because of a lack of raw materials, and the Nazis decided on a more radical solution than the one proposed by Schacht: they would emphasize economic self-sufficiency and reduce their dependency on foreign markets. This program came to be know as the Four-Year Plan.

THE FOUR-YEAR PLAN

In August 1936, Hitler ushered in the Four-Year Plan with a secret memo. In it, he called for the accomplishment of two basic tasks. First, the economy was to be prepared for war within four years. He then spelled out what that meant: a solution to the fuel problem within eighteen months, the mass production of synthetic rubber, the immediate expansion of the iron and steel industry, a heightened effort to produce metals from low-grade ores, the development of more light metals, and a stepped-up production of nonanimal fats. Second, the German armed forces were to be ready for war within four years.

The memo did not exactly state that war was to be expected within that time, only that the military and the economy were to be ready. It is also clear that, except for fuels and rubber, Hitler did not expect complete self-sufficiency within the time frame but expected moves in that direction and a decreased dependency on foreign resources. Hitler further stipulated that he considered the Four-Year Plan a temporary expedient. "The definitive solution," he wrote, "lies in an extension of our living space, that is, an extension of the raw materials and food basis of our nation."[1] In other words, now that the economy was recovering, armaments and possible expansion were to be emphasized even more than before.

In September, Hitler publicly announced the Plan and appointed Göring to oversee its implementation. This put Schacht at a definite disadvantage, for he continued to favor more orthodox means of dealing with Germany's economic problems, such as maintaining the stability of the currency, and he did not approve of financing new initiatives for raw materials production unless the projects were economically viable. But Hitler and Göring wanted to push rearmament and war preparations at a faster pace, so in September 1937, Schacht resigned as Minister of Economics and General Plenipotentiary of the War Economy, though not officially until the end of November. He

---

1 Quoted in Berenice A. Carroll, *Design for Total War: Arms and Economics in the Third Reich* (The Hague, 1968), 102.

held on to the presidency of the Reichsbank into 1939, but he did so with almost no influence on the nation's economic policies. Schacht was yet another example of an old German conservative whose political philosophy had led him to collaborate with Hitler but whose social snobbery and belief that he could control the Führer brought about his undoing. His eventual successor in both of his former positions was the more amenable Nazi, Walter Funk.

At about the same time, Hitler also decided to remove other conservative ministers and army leaders whom he felt might question his authority. Consequently, among others, the Foreign Minister, Konstantin von Neurath, the War Minister, Werner von Blomberg, and the army chief, Werner von Fritsch, were relieved of their posts. Hitler appointed the party "expert," Joachim von Ribbentrop, to head the foreign office, and in the case of the military, he dissolved the War Ministry and set up an Armed Forces High Command with himself in charge. The more pliable Walter von Brauchitsch was named commander-in-chief of the army. Hitler's control over all aspects of the state and economy was thus strengthened.

This "purge" further relieved some of the tensions that had built up between the governmental ministries and the army on the one hand, and the party and the Labor Front on the other. The ministries and the army wanted to concentrate all resources on rearmament and to keep wages down, while the party and the Labor Front wanted to maintain worker confidence by pushing for wage increases. Hitler desired both more arms and improved worker morale, so the issue was never completely resolved. In the end, however, labor shortages meant better wages for the workers no matter what position the various sides within the regime took.

Despite the priorities set out in the Four-Year Plan, the inefficiencies in the economic system became increasingly manifest after 1936. The Plan imposed another layer of administration on the economy, and even though state and party officials and representatives of private industry generally dominated the new organization, rival groups, such as the armed services, the Food Estate, the Labor Front, and the SS, were now also allowed to have a say in running the economy. This meant that there was no proper system of raw materials allocations, industrial investment remained largely unplanned, and firms competed against one another for lucrative governmental contracts. It was not an efficient system.

Nevertheless, the economy did move ahead. Those segments of industry related to Four-Year–Plan priorities usually benefitted most. Karl Krauch, a leading figure in I.G. Farben, took over the development of synthetic fuels and rubber, and the chemical firm received an almost unbelievable 72.7 percent of the total capital invested by the Four-Year Plan between 1936 and 1939. The state-sponsored Hermann Göring Iron Works started slowly in the processing of low-grade ore, but over the years it became an industrial giant involved not only in mining but in the production of machinery and even in shipping as well. The coal industry was not as fortunate, though it finally moved into liquid-fuel production and electric power and continued to be the primary supplier of energy for German industry. More dynamic was the automobile industry. The number of cars and trucks manufactured in Germany trebled between 1928 and 1938, and the consumption of oil products doubled during the same period.

Other areas of the economy also did well. Some of the governmental measures, as in calling for the electrification of homes, helped civilians. Some of them, as in the construction of the West Wall fortifications in western Germany, assisted the military. And others, as in the promotion of new production techniques for such items as rubber goods, artificial silk, plastics, and cellulose, benefitted both. In addition, the synthetics boom led to the building of new factories in south central Germany and stimulated the economy in that region. A more negative aspect was business involvement in buying out Jewish firms, a trend which accelerated in the late 1930s and left many Jews impoverished.

In agriculture, the situation was mixed. Göring and Four-Year–Plan officials had declared a battle for production in October 1936, and the amount of farm goods being produced did rise from 70 to more than 80 percent of domestic needs by 1939. This brought about a decline in farm imports, but there were still problems. The deficiency in fats could not be overcome, the large gap in the sector's need for fodder for feeding animals was only partially closed, farm mechanization suffered because iron and steel was being diverted from the construction of farm implements to armaments production, and the plans for land reclamation never started because of a lack of funds. An even greater problem was the exodus from the land. As early as 1935, the government again began allowing foreign laborers to be hired for farm work. Their numbers, which did not take into account numerous illegal seasonal workers from eastern Europe, still rose officially from 50,000 in 1936 to over 100,000 three years later. In addition, farmers had to depend more than ever on Labor Service personnel and boy and girl volunteers from the youth organizations to help plant and harvest the crops. Sufficient labor was simply not available to perform all of the necessary jobs in the agricultural sector.

Industrial workers were also caught up in the contradictory tendencies that characterized Nazi economic policies during the late 1930s. The government wanted prices and wages to remain low, but with the burgeoning economy and full employment, employers continued to skirt wage freezes by paying workers more through bonuses and "indirect" means. Increased wages and benefits coupled with scarcities in certain consumer items, such as margarine and shoes, tended to drive up prices. In June 1938, the regime finally decided to clamp down on the wage problem by prohibiting further increases, but the prohibition proved unenforceable, and wages rose, though more slowly, into the war itself. (One company instituted an ingenious method for circumventing the wage freeze by providing workers with motorcycles to transport themselves to and from work.)

The party and government also moved into transportation. To control labor mobility, Göring, also in June 1938, decreed that workers could be compulsorily shifted to jobs considered essential by the state. To raise productivity, the state started promoting the idea of paying workers piece-work instead of hourly wages. Both of these measures aroused labor resentment to such an extent that productivity was hurt, so in November 1939 Hitler declared that workers would no longer be forced to leave their hometowns to assume other jobs.

Working-class attitudes during this period are difficult to access. Some workers, especially those in the armaments factories, were undoubtedly better off than they had been in the

Weimar years. Others, like those in consumer goods industries and in agriculture, were worse off. In all, actual weekly wages rose 23 percent, or at an annual rate of 2.9 percent, between 1932 and 1939, but wages as a percentage of the gross national product declined during the same period from 57 to 51.8 percent. Furthermore, much of the raises were a result of overtime work rather than normal increases in weekly pay scales. In addition, there were examples of worker discontent in the form of strikes, slow-downs, and absenteeism, though not on the scale experienced at the same time in France and the United States. Still, it was better to be overworked than unemployed, and unemployment had nearly vanished. Only 35,000 of a total male work force of 25,000,000 were out of work in the summer of 1939. To overcome the labor shortages, foreign workers were brought into industry as they had been on farms (a total of 435,000 in March 1939), the government had undertaken large-scale retraining and apprenticeship programs (involving 1.2 million persons), and concentration camp labor was contracted to manufacturing firms.

The party was involved in labor activities in other ways. Labor Front staffs in the factories expanded and included persons to assist the workers in a variety of concerns from career counseling and health to job protection and leisure. They further gave special aid to Germans temporarily unemployed or injured on the job, functions formerly provided by the unions. Though only partially applicable to labor, the party's Welfare Agency undermined the religious and governmental relief organizations by taking over some child care, kindergarten, and preventive health care programs. It also assumed adoption services in parts of the country, even though the adoptions were based on a strict racial criteria.

The Nazi drive for a strong economy was tied in with foreign expansion during the late 1930s. The occupation of Austria in March 1938 enabled the Göring works to start using Austrian iron ore, which was superior to the low-grade ore they had been using. In September the Munich crisis resulted in Germany taking over the Sudetenland, and the following March, the entire Bohemian and Moravian portions of Czechoslovakia (Slovakia became a protectorate) came under Nazi control. Economically, the newly incorporated areas yielded coal, steel plants, and the

Skoda armaments works. Both Austria and Czechoslovakia also provided additional food for the Reich, thereby alleviating some of the shortages in agricultural products. Therefore, while neither of the takeovers required military action, the new territories proved to be valuable additions in terms of raw materials, finished products, and personnel available for use by the Wehrmacht, or Nazi military forces. Having whetted his appetite for more living space, Hitler now began plans for new ventures, despite signs of reticence on the part of the population at home. Germany had once again become the most feared nation in Europe.

How had Germany achieved such prominence economically? How had it raised the necessary capital? Part of the answer is found in its control of investment. The government reserved the capital market for its own long-term borrowing and restricted the private sector to self-financing and short-term borrowing. It also raised corporate tax rates by 5 percent per year after 1935 until it reached 40 percent in 1939, and it limited the amount of stock businesses and banks could issue and the percentage of dividends they could pay to stockholders, thereby encouraging companies to reinvest profits back into their industries. Finally, through a licensing scheme, it prohibited firms from expanding without governmental approval, which helped the Nazis drive the economy into what they wanted, namely war-related enterprises. In return, many industries made healthy profits (excess profits were turned over to the state), and the government generally kept labor and consumer demands under control by adjusting individual taxes and by retaining wage and price restraints.

Yet Germany's economic situation worsened during 1938–39. Forced rearmament and economic contradictions had created an overheated economy. Raw materials and skilled-labor shortages were becoming critical, mounting governmental expenditures were causing inflationary pressures, and the foreign exchange and balance-of-payments problem was again raising its head. But whether these economic difficulties pushed Hitler into war, as has been contended, is doubtful. The Four-Year Plan had helped in the drive toward self-sufficiency, but the Nazis had never expected that it would bring about complete self-sufficiency. The currency exchange crisis was serious, but it could be handled by redistributing and balancing the country's re-sources, and inflationary tendencies could be dampened by keeping down wages and prices. More important, Hitler never let economic problems stand in the way of his political goals. He no longer thought it necessary to postpone war. In fact, he might have gone to war earlier over the Rhineland remilitarization in 1936 or over Austria or Czechoslovakia in 1938 had he been forced to do so. When the war broke out over Poland in September 1939, it had been determined more by military and foreign policy considerations than by the state of the German economy.

By 1939, Germany was positioning itself for war, but it did not possess a total war economy. The production of items for civilian consumption had been reduced, but many goods were still available. Hitler also had a number of nonmilitary schemes in mind. He was planning to produce Volkswagens, refurbish the railroads, and erect large, prestigious buildings, monuments to the Third Reich, in such cities as Berlin and Nuremberg. Moreover, the country still had to depend on outside sources for some of its food and more than half of its oil, rubber, iron ore, and metals, such as lead, copper, tin, nickel, and aluminum bauxite.

Nevertheless, the National Socialists had placed enormous resources into building up the German military. The increase in the production of war materials was impressive.

German Selected War Materials
(Thousands of Tons)[2]

	1936	1939
Iron Ore	2,259	3,928
Aluminum	95	194
Aircraft Gasoline	43	302
Regular Gasoline	1,214	1,633
Synthetic Rubber	1	22

As can be seen in the table above, the rise in synthetic rubber and airplane gasoline was particular dramatic, but the vol-

2 Avraham Barkai, *Nazi Economics: Ideology, Theory and Policy* (New York, 1990), 230.

ume of other war-related products also increased. In addition, certain metals, such as nickel and copper, were not allowed to be used in consumer goods industries, and large scrap metal drives were already bring launched in an effort to reduce the importation of foreign raw materials. To be sure, in 1939 Germany was still devoting only 23 percent of its gross national product to military expenditures, but whereas RM 1.9 billion had been spent on the military in 1933, RM 17 billion had been spent in 1938, and an even more extensive construction program of ships and airplanes was inaugurated at the beginning of 1939. By the time the war had started on September 1, the army had 103 fully equipped divisions and 3,200 tanks, the air force 3,046 operational aircraft, and the navy, though less formidable, had 56 submarines and 6 pocket battleships in its inventory. Among the European powers, only the Soviet armed forces could match the Wehrmacht in total numbers, but whether they could match the Germans in quality of material or personnel is extremely doubtful.

At this point, the Nazi economy had evolved into a combination of private and state capitalism. Like the National Socialist political system, the economy featured numerous overlapping jurisdictions and contradictions, but Western capitalism never has been characterized as being overly streamlined. The Nazis did not do away with capitalism. They had intruded into the economy with the blessing of business and industry and the military and had, at first, shared power with them to an extent. But then in 1936, the Nazis had embarked on a more radical course. Business and the military had not disagreed with increased rearmament and had, in fact, willingly participated, but the government and the party became more heavily involved in the economy than ever before. They increasingly controlled and dominated it, but they did not abolish the private sector. Hitler and the Nazis had used capitalism to move the economy in the direction they wanted.

THE INTENTIONALIST-FUNCTIONALIST CONTROVERSY

Did the Nazis really control the German economy? Or did they actually lose control, and did this loss of control in the economic sphere ultimately push Germany into World War II? The extent to which Hitler and his entourage determined the events that led to the conflict and the extent to which they dominated the German agenda has caused a debate, known as the intentionalist-functionalist controversy, among historians for several decades. Although few historians are exclusively in the intentionalist or functionalist camp, the intentionalists, who are more traditional, contend that Hitler's ideas and actions, in other words, his "intentions," directly determined the direction of the Third Reich. His program was based on race, expansion, and war, and essentially he adhered to this program throughout his life. In the intentionalist view, Hitler's ideological obsessions eventually became governmental policy.

While not downplaying Hitler's crucial role, the functionalists concentrate more on how the Nazis "functioned," on the structure and nature of the polycratic state, the complicity of Germany's conservative elite, and the absence of a clear and consistent direction from Hitler himself. He knew what he wanted to destroy—the Jews, the left, and other enemies—but he often vacillated when it came to exercising his power. In fact, his indecisiveness, except in matters upholding his prestige and personal authority, has led several historians to assert that in some respects he was a weak dictator.

The functionalists point to Hitler's weakness, or inability to control events, not only in the economic realm, but also in the political, and even to a degree in matters of foreign and racial policies. From a political standpoint, Hitler's fragmented government was a result of his charismatic leadership, which led to a rejection of the usual bureaucratic norms one associates with running a government. Instead, Hitler ruled through propagandistic methods that precluded his interfering in the internal conflicts, and these conflicts gave rise to numerous contradictions within the Nazi state. In foreign affairs, the functionalists do not deny that Hitler made the major decisions, but they believe that domestic difficulties, such as labor discontent, shortages of food and raw materials, and a general lack of efficiency, forced the Führer to seek a military solution at the time he did. In the area of racial cleansing, functionalist historians do not take issue with Hitler's moral responsibility for the Holocaust, but they view him as a remote figure who determined the objective and shaped the climate but who was seldom directly involved.

For many historians, the functionalist approach is overdrawn, although their focus on the many pressures that built up inside Hitlerian Germany provide valuable insights into the dynamics of the Third Reich. Nazi Germany consisted of more than Hitler's will or his intentions, although they were crucial components. Other elements, such as the military, the industrialists, and to an extent the German bureaucracy as well as party leaders accepted his views and played a role in shaping the events that propelled Germany toward war. Hitler did not act alone; he had assistance. In this sense, both the intentionalist and the functionalist interpretations help deepen our understanding of the Nazi state.

4 / SOCIETY, CULTURE, AND
FOREIGN POLICY, 1933–1939

SOCIAL POLICY

Even though Nazi social policy was more consistent than its political and economic counterparts, it was still filled with contradictions. These contradictions stemmed from the inherent difference between the Nazis' long-term and short-term objectives. In the long run, Hitler and his associates believed in a racial elite, consisting of those fit to rule, set up so that all good Germans would some day enjoy the benefits of a comprehensive welfare system. This new state would eventually assure that the former elite—the aristocrats, the manufacturers, the bureaucracy—would be put in its place and diminished in stature. However, in the short run, and for practical reasons, Hitler was not interested in tampering with the existing social order.

The result was a deep chasm between what the Nazis said they believed in and what they actually did. They professed a revolutionary course, the establishment of a traditional yet modern state based on technological innovation, one which would take into account all of the German people, not just an elite based on a combination of class, education, and occupation. But they never reached this stage, and the society they envisaged would not have been truly modern in any event, but antimodern in the sense that economic betterment was to be used to prepare for war, and their racial policy was never intended for all the people, only for the German Volk. That so many Germans accepted this self-serving thinking may be understandable, but it is still not easy to forgive. To be sure, the Nazis developed their own symbols, their own songs, flags, and holidays, and they controlled communications through propaganda to such an extent that it was difficult for the population to distinguish truth from falsehoods. And while Nazi policies for dominating youth, relegating women to child-bearing and the home, undercutting the churches, and annihilating Jews and others not considered racially fit may have had their adherents, there were people in Germany, who, for one reason or another, opposed such policies. Their opposition may not have forced the Nazis to abandon their ultimate goal of a racially pure state, but it did lead to inconsistencies that persuaded Hitler and his followers not to move too rapidly. Examples of Nazi social policy abound, but four areas that demonstrate the variety and invidious nature of their policies are those toward youth, women, the churches, and race.

YOUTH

According to Hitler, young German people must be "tough as leather, and as hard as Krupp steel."[1] They were to fit into the heroic mold, and the National Socialists placed great emphasis on the proper training of youth, for the young held the keys to the future. The regime's efforts were not misplaced, in that it has been estimated that as many as 95 percent of the German youth backed the Nazis, or at least Hitler, and that opposition for the most part remained vague and diffuse.

Although Nazi thinking permeated every aspect of young people's lives, from education at all levels to out-of-school activities, the National Socialist programs were filled with contradictions, and these contradictions were never more evident than at the universities. At first, the Nazis wanted fewer students in the country, in part because the depression had made it difficult for graduates to find jobs in already overcrowded fields, in part because of the Nazis' antiintellectual bias. During the late 1930s, as the economy improved dramatically, the government desired more university graduates, but this proved impossible because of the demands of the armed services.

Also, by this point, the antiintellectual atmosphere had taken its toll, especially as related to the faculties of the universities. The civil service law of April 1933 had resulted in 1,145, or nearly

---

1 Max Domarus, ed. *Hitler: Speeches and Proclamations 1932–1945* Vol. 1 (Wauconda, Ill., 1990), 533.

15 percent, of the university-level teachers, being dismissed, approximately 33 percent for racial and 56 percent for political reasons. The purged scholars received little support from their colleagues. In November 1933, the professors signed a "Declaration in Support of Hitler and the National Socialist State," and one highly respected philosopher, Martin Heidegger, declared that the Führer was the present and future reality for Germany. Moreover, although Nazi ideology was too amorphous to replace the traditional curriculum in many areas, racial and eugenic ideas spread into medical studies, and law and political science courses were adapted to state policies. Scientists retreated into their narrow specialties, which, more often than not, were government-related. A lack of breadth and tolerance became the norm in university life.

This attitude filtered down to the students. Academic standards fell as National Socialist activities took up more and more of the students' time, so that eventually those who might have gone on for graduate work were often unprepared. It is not clear how much the Nazi student group, the Student League, contributed to this decline. The Student League had already taken over the leadership of the main student organization, the German Student Association, by the time of the Nazi takeover, and membership in the larger body became compulsory for full-time students early on. While some did resist the programs of the student organization, which featured regimentation, conformity, and antiintellectualism, many students obviously accepted National Socialism, though they seemed to want to do so in their own way.

The decrease in the number of registered students at universities was precipitous, from 113,245 in the summer of 1933, to 56,557 in the summer of 1939. During the war, the numbers rose again to a high of 82,495 in the summer of 1944. Although this total was still insufficient, an interesting point is that the proportion of female students increased, from 11.2 percent in the summer of 1939 to 49.3 percent in summer the of 1944. Women also began to invade the traditional "men's" disciplines, such as law, architecture, and the sciences, and there were also more female medical and humanities students than there had been before. Nazi promotion of women into higher education was not based on any change of policy, but it became apparent that for professional reasons they were needed.

National Socialist penetration of the high schools and grade schools was even more pervasive than it was at the university level. All teachers were to be ideologically reliable, and to ensure this, in February 1933, Hitler appointed a former schoolteacher and the Gau leader of Hanover-South Brunswick, Bernhard Rust, Minister of Culture (and later Minister of Education). Rust proceeded to establish committees, popularly known as "murder committees," to look into the political reliability of local teachers. In addition, the small National Socialist Teachers' League was to assist Rust by reporting whether or not individual teachers had the proper Nazi outlook before they were appointed or promoted to new positions. By 1936–37, league membership had jumped to 320,000, or 97 percent of the active teachers, and it had been put in charge of the teachers' political indoctrination.

Rust's ministry soon became the dominant force in education. In January 1935, all state ministries of culture were directed to carry out the regulations of his national education office, and the ministry was also to approve all textbooks. School curriculum was to emphasize physical exercise and National Socialist ideas. Though the physical sciences and math were generally untouched by Nazi ideology, in biology and history the situation was different. Biology was now to deal extensively with the Nazis' racial theories, and history courses were to focus on the glories of Nordic culture and great leaders, such as Caesar, Charlemagne, and Frederick the Great.

Boys and girls were to be separated at the high-school level because of the different functions the sexes were expected to perform in society. This design was never fully realized, however, and some girls continued to attend boys' schools throughout the period. Still, most girls went to girls' high schools, and their curriculum was altered to reflect the Nazi outlook. During the first three years of secondary education, girls were to take needlework and music instead of Latin, and during the last three they were to study language or home crafts. No provisions were made to instruct them in math or science: their role as homemakers and mothers was to be emphasized.

Nevertheless, Rust's control was less than complete. The Teachers' League appeal was limited, especially when teachers learned that Hitler cared little about their issues and thought that retired army sergeants would make excellent elementary teachers. Furthermore, Rust himself was a weak man who was unable to protect education from the intervention of ambitious party leaders, including, among others, Schirach, Bormann (Hitler's secretary), Ley, Himmler, and Goebbels.

Special National Socialist schools, founded to produce the hoped for new elite, well illustrate Rust's problem. In 1933, he established National Political Education Institutes, or Napolas, for males ten-to-eighteen years old. The Napolas were to educate the future officer corps and thus develop the proper military values—courage, honor, discipline—among the students. Eventually thirty-nine such schools were formed, but during 1936 they were actually put under the direction of the SS, and only nominally under Rust.

Rust was not even involved in two other Nazi educational experiments, the Adolf Hitler and Ordensburgen schools. In 1937, Schirach and Ley instituted the Adolf Hitler schools for twelve-to-eighteen-year-olds. These were free boarding-schools that stressed military training and political indoctrination as befitted future party leaders. The Ordensburgen, or Order Castles, were founded by Ley in the mid-1930s as "finishing" schools for individuals with extensive party experience, and like the Hitler and Napola schools, they were designed to develop a person's intuition rather than his intellect. None of the three— and Alfred Rosenberg envisioned a fourth, a National Socialist university, which never really got started—were adequate alternatives to regular schooling. As evidence, almost none of the party leaders sent their own children to any of these schools, and Bormann sent one of his sons to an Adolf Hitler school as a punishment.

During the early years of the Third Reich, Protestant and Catholic schools still played a significant role in German elementary and, to an extent, secondary education. At first they continued to function normally, but the state soon began to intervene with various regulations, and in the summer of 1939, all denominational schools were abolished.

Another exceedingly interesting example of alternative schooling—and of Nazi contradictions—were the Jewish schools. The April 1933 law that limited the proportion of Jewish students who could attend regular schools prompted the opening of these separate Jewish institutions. Although the total number of Jewish children who went to these schools declined as increasing numbers of Jews left the country, in December 1937, there were still 23,670, or 60 percent, of the eligible Jewish children enrolled in Jewish schools. When, eleven months later, the government forced those Jews who remained in the state schools to leave, the children moved over to their own schools. Despite continual discrimination and harassment, the last Jewish school was not closed until July 1942.

While Nazi authorities were heavily involved in the schools, traditional features of the educational system still tended to limit the party's influence. There were, however, no such restrictions on out-of-school activities. Since the Nazi goal was to make German youth into good National Socialists, influences outside the party, including even those of the family, were to be minimized. At the age of ten the process began with the assimilation of young people, as fully as possible, into the Hitler Youth. Then, at age eighteen, they were to move into the Labor Service, and then they were to enter the military or volunteer for party work.

The Hitler Youth was the key organization. It was divided into four separate groups. For males, ten-to-fourteen-year-olds were in the Young Boys division, fourteen-to-eighteen-year-olds were in the Hitler Youth. Ten-year-old females became members of the Young Girls division, and fourteen-year-olds entered the League of German Girls. Although few chose to do so, participation by young women in the League of German Girls could be extended to age twenty-one by joining its Faith and Beauty Organization. By the end of 1933, all youth groups, except Catholic and Jewish groups, had been disbanded or amalgamated into the Hitler Youth. In 1936, it reached the next stage: all German young people were "encouraged" to become members of the Nazi groups. Despite propaganda and pressure to get all young people to enroll voluntarily, the youth leaders were not satisfied with the results, so membership became compulsory in March 1939. It is estimated that at that time most young people, around 82 percent of the total, were affiliated with one of the Hitler Youth groups.

Its oath, "I promise to do my duty in the Hitler Youth at all times, in love and loyalty to the Führer," helps explain the direction of its activities. It set up its own newspapers, magazines, theater groups, and radio shows to expand its appeal. Camping and hiking excursions took on a political orientation with prescribed sessions to extol Nazi virtues. The Hitler Youth also sponsored an annual national Skills and Performance Competition, in which youths were to test their technical and craft skills against others in various areas, such as agriculture, construction, and textiles. By 1939, adults were taking part with 3½ million people competing. The activity proved so popular that Hitler Youth also began to hold an annual national Sports Competition.

During the war, the Hitler Youths' activities took on an even more patriotic cast. In late 1939, every Hitler Youth boy and most girls were directed to perform "land service" each year to help harvest the crops. All of the older males were also subject to "youth service," a type of premilitary training held on Sunday mornings, despite objections from the churches. Beginning in 1943, Hitler Youth formed work battalions and furnished personnel for defensive positions, such as antiaircraft batteries. And late in the war, it signed up volunteers for the *Volkssturm*, the pitiful youth corps instituted by Hitler to fight the enemy.

In spite of the pressure to conform to Hitler Youth precepts, some youths evaded service. They became only nominal members who paid their dues, but they had notes from their doctors describing health problems, or from their teachers, claiming that they had academic difficulties and therefore could not participate. Others simply did not show up at meetings, although evasion became harder after the war broke out.

Some young people went further and formed their own groups. They were part of the wandering youth tradition that had grown up in nineteenth-century Germany, and they were bored with National Socialist dogma and wanted to do things on their own. Groups of working-class youth known as, among other names, Edelweiss Pirates sprung up in various cities. They consisted of fourteen-to-eighteen-year-olds, mostly males, who gathered at local bars and made weekend trips into the surrounding countryside, where they camped out, talked, and sang songs (often with anti-Nazi lyrics). Other working-class groups, called packs, resembled the Edelweiss Pirates, but they espoused Communist themes, such as the violent overthrow of the government, and thus were more politically motivated. Less ideological were the upper-middle-class Swing groups. These young people had the money to frequent nightclubs, where they danced the jitterbug, and they bought and played phonograph records featuring American and British music. All three groups were repressed by the police and even thrown into jail on occasion, but they were seldom persecuted since they were needed as workers or future soldiers. The pirates, packs, and swing groups might not have liked the Hitler Youth, but they were not a real threat to the regime.

WOMEN

No area of everyday German life was more susceptible to contradictions than that of the role of women. The main problem for the Nazis was the distinction between theory and practice. In theory, they recognized that women were vital to the health of the community, and they were to fulfill their role primarily by being wives and mothers. Hitler and his associates insisted that men and women occupied separate spheres and that this should be recognized and developed for the good of the nation. Women were not inferior but should confine themselves to areas in which they could exhibit their "natural" qualities, such as compassion and self-sacrifice, and they should not display "unnatural" attributes, such as independence and a competitive spirit. In other words, women should remain in the home, raise children, and support their husbands.

In practice the situation was quite different. The Nazis tried to impose their beliefs, but for years some women had been employed outside the home, many in a blue-collar environment, such as in the textile and clothing industries. Some women were also doctors, lawyers, and other professionals, and they were not anxious to return merely to the three German K's—children, church, and cooking—for they had obviously found other means of fulfillment. More important, as was mentioned, the Nazis themselves, by the late 1930s, realized that they required more women in the work force to help in their preparations for war. They had never really opposed women working, particularly single women, so long as the jobs they performed were related to the type of work that women did best—grade school teaching, nursing, social work. But now women were needed for factory work as well as for the professions. The problem for the Nazis now was that after having received incentives to stay at home and having been subjected to so much Nazi propaganda about the sanctity of homelife, women were reluctant to take on additional jobs. Therefore the Nazis, trapped in another contradiction, had to turn to other means, such as the importation of foreign workers, in order to fulfill their labor requirements. German women did aid in the war as volunteers in hospitals and by organizing groups to send goods to the soldiers, but they did not participate sufficiently in the ways the Nazis wanted. In a sense, the Nazis' propaganda had succeeded too well.

One of the major reasons that the National Socialists promoted marriage and family life was that they wanted German, or at least Aryan, women to have more children. Since Germany had had a declining birth rate during the Weimar period, the Nazis introduced a number of measures to reverse that trend. One was the marriage loan program instituted in June 1933. According to the scheme, a couple of German nationality was loaned 1,000 marks. They were paid in vouchers, which were to be used to buy furniture and other household goods from approved stores. The key provision was that though the loan was to be repaid, for every child the couple had, one-fourth of the interest-free loan would be forgiven, so that if a couple had four children, their loan would be considered completely paid off. Furthermore, the wife, who had to have been working prior to the loan, would have to agree to give up her job and not go back to work, so long as the husband was employed, until the loan had been repaid. When the Nazis reversed themselves in 1936–37 and decided to encourage women to work outside the home, the prohibition on the employment provision was dropped.

The Nazis also undertook other measures to encourage procreation. In October 1934, the government provided couples with several additional incentives to have children, such as increasing maternity benefits and doubling the income-tax deduction for dependent children. The next year they introduced family allowances, which granted large, poor families an average of RM 100 per child per year. Prior to the war, they came up with another promotional scheme. On every Mother's Day, German mothers who had four children or more were to be presented crosses of honor. The metal used for the crosses depended on the number of children: for mothers who had four or five children, the cross was bronze; for those who had six or seven, it was silver; for those with eight or more, it was gold. As a final touch, on the back of each cross was the inscription, "The child ennobles the Mother!"

The extent to which the various Nazi measures encouraged people to have more children is difficult to assess. The incentives were popular, and the birth rate did rise, from fifty-nine births per thousand women of child-bearing age in 1933 to eighty-five per thousand in 1939. But better economic conditions may have had more to do with the increase than did the governmental inducements.

Two other governmental policies—toward divorce and abortion—also had an impact, though minimal, on the party's desire to produce more children for the Reich. Divorce was made easier, particularly if the grounds were infertility or a lack of desire of one of the partners to have children. When it came to abortions, the situation was more complicated. The Nazis agreed with the antiabortion laws that had been passed during the Weimar period and tried to see that they were strictly enforced. Persons who performed abortions on healthy German women, except for medical reasons, were subject to up to two years' imprisonment, and, during the war, the law was extended to include the death penalty in some cases. But the Nazis did approve of abortion in certain instances. Women deemed racially inferior or severely retarded were encouraged to have abortions, and the official attitude toward abortion for unwed mothers became less restrictive as time went on. Early in 1939, the government instructed its offices that female employees should not be dismissed simply because they had given birth to an illegitimate child. During the war, the party started awarding unmarried women the same RM 100 per child grant as married women, and the government gave grants to unwed mothers who required support, thereby acknowledging that there could be exceptions to the abortion rules so long as more German children were produced.

The Nazi promotion of home values did not preclude women performing outside employment. Even during the early years of the regime, when unemployment was high and the encouragement of women to remain at home strongest, there were certain realities that the government could not ignore. As a result of World War I, there were approximately two million more women than men in Germany. Many women did not get married and had to support themselves and often dependents as well. Even though few women succeeded in gaining middle- or upper-level positions, many desired work for financial reasons. The government realized that these reasons justified some flexibility on their part, so they accepted women's employment, again provided that their work was concentrated in "natural occupations" and did not strain the women physically. Still, female employment was low during the period, declining from 35.4 percent of the labor force in 1933 to 31.3 percent in 1936, though, again, much of the explanation lies not so much in Nazi policies as in the fact that the economic recovery took place largely in the production goods sector and not in the consumer goods sector, where most women were employed.

As noted, the government's change of attitude took place in 1936–37 with increased rearmament and the resulting labor shortage. Women were now to be both mothers and workers, and the percentage of female workers in the labor force did rise to 36.7 percent in 1939, but this percentage was still short of what the Nazis wanted and needed.

Therefore, during the war, Nazi policies toward female employment were a strange mixture. To encourage women to work, day nurseries were established and social workers hired to counsel female factory workers about family problems. But, at the same time, women also experienced disincentives to work. While some of the new jobs that women held were relatively pleasant, such as positions as ticket collectors or conductors on streetcars or trains or as post office clerks, the factory work that many women performed was often unpleasant and fatiguing and entailed long shifts. Nor was the one year of compulsory labor service for young women popular, since it involved primarily agricultural field work or domestic service. Furthermore, widows of servicemen received generous housing allowances and additional allowances for children. These subsidies persuaded many women to remain at home, and these subsidies were not in any danger of being cut, for fear of damaging soldiers' and sailors' morale.

The result of these mixed policies was that the percentage of women in the work force rose but not dramatically until 1939–40, when it reached 40 percent of the total. It then hovered at that figure throughout the rest of the conflict. There were mitigating factors. No German women served in the military, but by 1944, the armed forces were employing 470,500 women, and of the 7 million foreign workers in Germany at this time, 1½ million were women. These factors merely underline the point that the Nazis' desire to place more women in blue-collar jobs was generally a failure.

They were more successful when it came to persuading women to work in the professions. Given their antiintellectual bias, the Nazis were prejudiced against women working in the professions, but they accepted the fact that women had been involved in professional jobs for some time and would not be easily removed. The primary Nazi concern was that women professionals remain loyal to the regime. Some German women were dismissed from public employment as a result of the civil service act of April 1933, but their removal was for political or racist reasons. In August 1936 Hitler decreed that in the future women would not be allowed to serve as judges or court attorneys, but this prohibition did not apply to those already serving in those capacities, and women lawyers, though small in number, were still not excluded from private practice or from becoming office administrators.

As had been the case with blue-collar workers, the actual governmental encouragement of women to become professionals started in 1936–37, and it accelerated the next year when officials realized that there were insufficient numbers of males to perform the many needed professional positions. The outcome was that more women were accepted into the universities, more became professionals, especially doctors and teachers, and some began to move into other areas that had been largely closed to them previously. Yet the regime considered the change a temporary expedient, one that it hoped could be rolled back once the war was won.

The various women's groups were caught up in these conflicting tendencies. Most of the conservative and bourgeois organizations offered little resistance to Nazi assimilation, and the two National Socialist groups followed the party program of promoting family life and motherhood. Moreover, the National Socialist groups were headed by a single person, Gertrud Scholtz-Klink. But this apparent unity was deceptive. Although Scholtz-Klink was the nominal leader, the Women's Bureau and the Women's Association were bourgeois-oriented and lacked the dynamism to have a major national impact. The larger Women's Bureau (about four million members) established a Reich Mothers' Service to train mothers to undertake tasks related to motherhood, and it offered courses in other domestic subjects, such as sewing, cooking, and child care. It also participated in volunteer work such as visiting with the sick and mending clothes for needy families. The smaller, and supposedly more elitist, Women's Association (with around two million members) also administered courses, including one on "racial science" to help women choose the proper, healthy, German partner.

However, the Women's Bureau and the Women's Association were generally ineffective in relating to the needs of working women. They switched their appeal in the late 1930s to emphasize both employment and home life, and the Bureau had a division in the Labor Front. However, the women's Labor Front office itself, under Alice Rilke, became more important in addressing the concerns of working women. Scholtz-Klink and the other leaders were too accepting of Nazi ideals that espoused a male-dominated society to become powerful advocates for women's issues.

However, before one condemns the women's organizations too much for their ineffectiveness, it is good to remember that at this time the situation in Germany was not that different from the situation in other industrial countries. Around the world, the number of women in the professions was relatively small, and they were paid less than men for comparable work. Most working women were in low-paying jobs with little opportunity for advancement, and many middle-class women did not work outside the home. Furthermore, many countries at the time discriminated against women of certain races, but the main difference between them and Nazi Germany is that other nations at least afforded women some protection under the law. In Germany, the law had been subverted to such an extent that it offered virtually no protection, though this distinction applied to all persons in German society.

THE CHURCHES

At first, Hitler's position toward the churches was one of tolerance. Although fundamentally hostile to Christianity, he had no clear policy on church-state relations when he assumed power in 1933. He was basically indifferent to theological questions, though he felt that Christianity was too closely tied to Judaism. He further believed that at some future date Nazi ideology would replace Christian dogma and become the bedrock of the new German society. And at this point his opposition to the churches was more political than ideological. It was the churches' power and influence that first needed to be diminished; their outmoded beliefs would be stripped away later.

Many leading church figures had welcomed the Nazi government. The Protestant churches were divided into two main denominations—Lutheran and Reformed Calvinist—as well as twenty-eight separate state churches, and many of them thought that the new regime would provide more centralized authority, of which they approved. The Catholics were more skeptical of the regime because of their traditional loyalty to the pope, but their fears were allayed somewhat by a Concordat signed by the German government and the papacy in July 1933. According to its provisions, the state guaranteed the right of free worship and the right to circulate pastoral letters and to maintain Catholic schools. In return, the Catholic church agreed to renounce all political activity within the Reich. In other words, its organizations were to confine themselves to religion and not become involved in political matters. Despite this agreement, the government continued to try to limit the Church's activities even further, and although some Catholic leaders (notably Cardinal Michael Faulhaber of Munich) protested, others were content not to voice their disapproval and went along with Nazi restrictions.

Support for nazism was not limited to the churches' hierarchies. Many individual ministers and priests agreed with the party's stance against communism and socialism and its espousal of German nationalism. A number of conservative theologians felt that modern society and its liberal tendencies were undermining traditional Christian values and thought that the National Socialists would reverse this trend. More radical was the German Christian movement. Founded in 1932, its proponents wanted the unification and nationalization of the Protestant church, with its revival and renewal being similar to that promised by Hitler for the state. The movement's leader, Joachim Hossenfelder, proclaimed that the German Christians were "the SA of the Church," and that they would lead the people spiritually in building the Third Reich. The German Christians convinced Hitler that a unified church would be beneficial to him, and he forced the election of a military chaplain and devoted Nazi, Ludwig Müller, as Reich chaplain. Müller began by placing German Christians into church offices.

The activities of the German Christians stirred opposition within the greater Protestant church, for the German Christians not only desired to unite the Protestant church along the lines of Hitler's leadership principle, they were also unquestioning in their support of the Führer and, more especially, of Nazi racial dogma. In September 1933, a number of Protestant pastors, led by the Berlin minister, Martin Niemöller, set up an Emergency League to combat what they viewed as the increased nazification of the church. By the beginning of 1934, the League had 4,000 members.

In April, this opposition became institutionalized in the form of what was called the Confessing Church. Besides Niemöller, its members included, among others, noted theologians Karl Barth and the brilliant, young Dietrich Bonhoeffer. In May, the Confessing Church met in the town of Barmen and issued a statement of principles. The Barmen Confessions stated that the views of the German Christians were incorrect and that state domination over the church in all matters was wrong. Nevertheless, the Confessing Church did not consider its statement to be political. Their main concern was religious. They thought the German Christians were subverting the purity of the gospels and the universality of the Christian message.

Nazi authorities did not look upon the Confessions in a similar light. They viewed the Barmen Confessions as an act of defiance, and they proceeded to arrest numerous Lutheran bishops throughout the country, but adverse reaction at home and abroad prompted Hitler to intervene. He realized that Müller and the German Christians had not brought about a unified Protestant church, so their adherents were replaced by more conservative church officials, who stayed aloof from state matters, and Müller, though retaining his office, was rendered ineffective.

Another factor in the demise of the German Christians was the attitude of the more radical elements in the party, such as Bormann, Goebbels, and Rosenberg. They had wanted a more aggressive policy against the churches from the start but had been held back by the Führer. They also did not want the German Christians to became a leading force in the party either, for they desired a new religion based on Nazi principles, not on Christianity. Although Hitler was not willing to go that far, from 1934–35 on, the regime stepped up its attacks on the churches. They did not want to move too fast, but they had three goals in mind. They wanted the state to gain administrative control first over the Protestant church, and then over the Catholic church. They desired to reduce the churches to insignificance, preferably through propaganda and intimidation but, if necessary, through widespread arrest and imprisonment of church leaders. And, as noted, they eventually wanted to establish a new cult to replace Christianity with a more up-to-date religion, National Socialism. While they never achieved any of these goals, partly because of their own inconsistencies, they made efforts in all three directions.

Even though Hitler had discarded Müller and the German Christians, he still wanted the churches under tighter state control, so he named another Nazi, Hans Kerrl, to head a newly created Ministry of Church Affairs. Kerrl, however, had little power, and he was resisted by the party radicals—Kerrl did not see nazism and Christianity as incompatible—and by the Confessing Church, which viewed his endeavors as an attempt to infuse the church with nazism.

Increasingly the government restricted the activities of church groups to "purely religious matters," and many went out of existence. The real power in the struggle against the churches, however, became vested more and more in the police and

Gestapo. When both the Protestant Confessing Church in 1936, and the Vatican, through a papal encyclical, *Mit brennender Sorge* (With Deep Anxiety), in 1937, condemned Nazi practices and their position toward race, the regime undertook a series of persecutions and trials that ended in the arrest and convictions of hundreds of Catholic priests and nuns, many on morals charges, and Protestant clergy, including Pastor Niemöller, on charges of various acts against the state. Niemöller was not convicted but was later arrested again and sent to several concentration camps, where he remained throughout the war. Allied soldiers liberated him at Dachau in 1945. A few others, such as Bonhoeffer, even helped Jews to escape Germany, and he was eventually imprisoned for his anti-Nazi activities and executed a month before the war ended.

Yet, during the late 1930s, Niemöller and Bonhoeffer were the exceptions. Clergy of both major faiths were persecuted and many imprisoned, but less than fifty for long terms. After the outbreak of the war, Hitler called a truce on antichurch activities to avoid increasing social tensions, though he still planned to do away with the established churches in the future. Even a person as radical as Goebbels agreed and said that wartime was simply not the right time to abolish the established churches. He added that Hitler had told him that if his (Hitler's) mother were alive, she would undoubtedly want to go to mass and he would not hinder her.

In the end, some clergy did actively resist the Nazis, and some, like Bonhoeffer and Father Alfred Delp, gave their lives after joining resistance movements that plotted to overthrow the regime, but their numbers were few. Many clergymen wholeheartedly backed the Nazi movement. They may have had reservations, but, if so, they seldom expressed them. It is difficult to account for the meager resistance of most clergy—though the overwhelming acceptance of nazism by their respective congregations and parishes, their distrust of leftist thinking, their own conservatism, their belief in the separation of political affairs from one's spiritual life, and their tradition of subservience to the state, as practiced in particular by Lutheranism—all played a part. Whatever the reason, the churches' overall response to National Socialism was timid and half-hearted and helped erode their influence on German life. An admission of the church self-guilt was brought out at a Protestant Church meeting in Stuttgart soon after the war. Its public statement read in part:

> We know ourselves to be one with our people in a great suffering and in a great solidarity of guilt. With great pain do we say: Through us endless suffering has been brought to many people and countries. . . . We accuse ourselves for not witnessing more courageously, for not praying more faithfully, for not believing more joyously, and for not loving more ardently [our fellow human beings.][2]

RACISM

Amidst all of the Nazi inconsistencies, one area in which they did demonstrate some consistency was in their racial policies. Hitler's anti-Semitism was deep and abiding. To be sure, the intensity with which the regime persecuted Jews varied over time—and the Nazis persecuted other elements besides Jews—but there is no doubt that Hitler and his followers believed that Jews should be removed from society, and many people in Germany went along. However, what few Germans could have perceived was that this policy of "removal" would eventually result in the murder of six million Jews.

Anti-Jewish policies and actions did not begin, of course, in Germany in 1933. Jews had been discriminated against for centuries. From the fourth century A.D., they had been expected to convert to Christianity. But when conversion did not prove overly successful, authorities turned to another policy, expulsion, and expulsion or exclusion remained the core of anti-Semitic thinking, even after it became associated with more virulent racial theories during the nineteenth century. And, in fact, even the National Socialists for a number of years adopted the policies of exclusion or expulsion. But by 1941, the Nazis found themselves in a total war. Expulsion was no longer possible. The Jewish problem had to be solved by other means, and the Nazis came up with another policy, the "final solution," or

---

2 Quoted in John S. Conway, *The Nazi Persecution of the Churches, 1933–1945* (New York, 1969), 332.

destruction process. All Jews—and other undesirables—were to be destroyed. This final stage, the destruction process, as brought out in the intentionalist-functionalist controversy, was not predetermined. Hitler was not determined to eliminate all Jews from the time he assumed power. As the Nazis saw it, it was a solution to a practical problem at the time, though they did not regret undertaking it, nor was the process inevitable. It did not have to happen, but it did, and history has never been the same.

The process consisted of a number of actions, many of which were overlapping. Five of them—discrimination, definition, expropriation, emigration, and concentration—were put into effect between 1933 and 1939. These actions continued to be used or expanded between 1939 and 1945, but during the war, three more came into being—mobile killing operations, concentration camps, and extermination camps. Together, they represent the Nazi attempt to eliminate the Jewish race.

Discrimination against Jews had started almost as soon as the National Socialists assumed power, and the number of restrictions was continually added to during the life of the regime. Some were merely frustrating, such as being excluded from memberships in sports clubs or not being allowed to shop except during certain hours or, after 1942, not being permitted to keep pets. (The pets were to be turned in to animal shelters and put to sleep, since they were "tainted" by Jewish blood.) Other measures were humiliating, such as being required to adopt the middle name of "Israel" or "Sarah," or being forced to wear a yellow, Jewish star, and others were exceedingly damaging, such as being excluded from the military, civil service, and other professions and being deprived of citizenship. But whether trivial or important, all of the Nazis' anti-Semitic policies had a serious effect on every Jewish person in the country.

Also meaningful were the Nuremberg Laws of September 1935. Not only did they forbid marriage and extramarital relations between Jews and German citizens, they also, after months of wrangling, set forth the definition of a Jew. According to the law, there were three types of Jews. The least Jewish, or mixed Jew (*Mischlinge*), was a mixed Jew of the second degree. This was a person with one Jewish grandparent. The next category was a *Mischlinge* of the first degree. This was a person with two Jewish grandparents, but who did not belong to the Jewish religion, or was not married to a Jew as of September 15. Both mixed Jews of the second or first degree were not to be persecuted. The final category was Jews. This was a person with three or four Jewish grandparents, or one with two Jewish grandparents and who belonged to the Jewish faith or was married to a Jew on September 15. The law did not stipulate what was to happen to this final group, but the definition formed the basis for further actions against Jews.

One of these actions was expropriation, or the Nazi effort to destroy Jewish wealth. It included various measures. The dismissal of Jews from jobs, of course, deprived those let go of their livelihood, as did the "Aryanization" of Jewish enterprises, by which Jews were forced to sell out to German firms. Then there was the high property tax on Jews who wanted to leave the country, the blocking of their money in banks, special Jewish taxes and wage regulations, and eventually food restrictions and forced labor for Jews. While these measures hurt even those Jews fortunate enough to emigrate, they left many who stayed destitute.

A real turning point in the state's treatment of Jews occurred during so-called Crystal Night, or the breaking of the glass of Jewish-owned property, on November 9, 1938. The origin of Crystal Night had taken place two days earlier, when a minor German official at the Paris embassy, Ernst von Rath, had been shot and killed by a disgruntled, Jewish youth, Herschel Grünspan. Goebbels, who was temporarily out of favor with Hitler because of an affair he had had with a Czech actress, used the occasion to get back into the Führer's good graces by advocating a looting of Jewish stores. SD and Gestapo chief Heydrich was directed to oversee the operation, and his agents proceeded to go on a rampage. They destroyed 7,500 Jewish businesses and homes, set fire to more than 200 synagogues, and murdered 91 Jews in the process. In addition, they arrested 26,000 Jews and put many of them into concentration camps. Most were released within several months, but only after they had given a written promise that they would leave the country. As a final indignity, on the basis that Jews had received insurance claims for their damaged property, Göring had them assessed an annual contribution of RM 1 billion for their "association" with the killing of von Rath.

Nazi "encouragement" of emigration was another important element of their policies toward Jews throughout the early period. Despite the financial restrictions and strong family attachments, many Jews desired to leave. This trend accelerated after Crystal Night. By May 1939, of the original 750,000 Jews who inhabited Germany and Austria, about 300,000, or less than half, remained. Of those whom emigrated, approximately 150,000 went to the United States, 70,000 to Palestine, and 230,000 to western Europe and elsewhere.

Those who stayed in Greater Germany (Germany, Austria, and the Czech lands) faced a further Nazi action, concentration. Actually, at first, the Jews voluntarily relocated. As they became more and more impoverished, they migrated to the cities where they could have the help of Jewish relief organizations and associate with their own communities. At this point it was only a short step to put the Jews into ghettos. This the German bureaucracy accomplished, particularly in Poland after the war began, since it figured that Jews would now be easier to control. These moves left the Jews who remained in the Greater Reich destitute, but an even worse fate, which will be examined in the next chapter, was to await them during the war that followed.

THE DEBASEMENT OF CULTURE

Nazi culture, both high and low, became concentrated in one person, Joseph Goebbels. Goebbels, it will be recalled, had directed the party propaganda machine for several years before being named the government's Minister of Popular Enlightenment and Propaganda in March 1933. A centralizer, Goebbels in September created the Reich Culture Chamber to carry out his wishes. It consisted of seven chambers—literature, music, radio, press, film, theater, and fine arts. These departments became further differentiated into numerous sections (the film chamber, for instance, had ten sections). Anyone active in the arts or media was forced to join the appropriate chamber and to agree to its regulations and guidelines. Non-Aryans and political "unreliables" were not admitted to membership.

Despite resistance from former ministries and agencies that had previously been responsible for cultural matters, and attempted encroachments from other party leaders such as Rosenberg and Ley, Goebbels was able to build a formidable empire. The individual chambers usually exercised control over their own areas, making sure that the output of writers, artists, musicians, journalists, broadcasters, and the like conformed to Nazi tastes and standards. The chamber did, however, have a more positive side. It sponsored projects for unemployed professionals, held workshops for aspiring dramatists and musicians, and instituted a social insurance system to assist its members.

Nevertheless, for the most part, the chambers' impact was negative. This may seem rather surprising, since Hitler was devoted to what he thought constituted high culture, and Goebbels and Göring had pretensions in the same direction, Göring as an art collector, and Goebbels as a writer and playwright. But Hitler's view of culture was selective. He wanted to promote an Aryan, traditional, heroic culture that every German could understand and believe in. He did not like the modern trends, such as German expressionism, which he considered ambiguous, distorted, and incoherent, and he wanted to protect society from these "degenerate" influences. His opinions, as executed by Goebbels and others, mark a low point in German cultural history.

In painting and sculpture, the Nazi view was particularly damaging. The experimentation that had characterized the Weimar period was reversed, and many of those artists' works were confiscated or removed from galleries. The famous school for painters and architects, the Bauhaus, was closed, and its inspirational leader, Walter Gropius, moved to the United States. Paul Klee, one of the Bauhaus's renowned teachers and an outstanding artist, was denounced as a Siberian Jew and also left the country, in his case to Switzerland. Between 1933 and 1945, over a thousand of Emil Nolde's paintings and watercolors were removed from German museums. During the same time, 381 of Ernst Barlach's sculptures were taken from churches and other buildings, and 4,000 copies of a volume of his drawings were confiscated and destroyed by the Gestapo. The equally famous Ernst Kirchner had been commissioned to design and paint several murals for a museum in Essen, but soon after the Nazis assumed power, museum officials ordered him to abandon the project. And the list could go on and on.

The public reaction to Nazi measures was not what they had hoped or expected it would be. In July 1937, with great fanfare, Goebbels and his cohorts opened a House of German Art in Munich to portray artistic works of the "true German creative spirit." But the paintings of farm life, landscapes, and female nudes (that depicted women's biological value) by second-rate artists, were uninspiring, and people soon lost interest in viewing them. By contrast, that same month an Exhibition of Degenerate Art also opened in Munich. Its modern paintings by Nolde, Klee, Kirchner, and "outsiders," such as Paul Gauguin and Pablo Picasso, were viewed by two million visitors before it closed four months later. After the exhibition, Goebbels tried to make sure that no more modern art was put on display in galleries or museums.

The Nazis' position toward another of Hitler's favorite topics, architecture, was more ambivalent. The Führer himself preferred big buildings and heroic monuments, and he and his state architect, Albert Speer, pored over architectural plans for hours in anticipation of redoing Berlin, Nuremberg, and his boyhood hometown, Linz, in Austria. But the reality was different from Hitler's grandiose plans. The National Socialists never developed a distinctive architectural style. They allowed buildings to be constructed in almost every style imaginable—neo-Romanesque (resembling the Middle Ages), neoclassical, rural (in the case of housing developments), and even modern. Although the central government assumed responsibility for building codes and other regulations, instead of state or municipal authorities, they did not dictate style as long as new buildings were functional. The Bauhaus buildings in Berlin, for instance, remained the same except that sloping wood roofs were added—they were converted into a school for party leaders. Hitler may have had a unified architectural style in mind, but it was put off because of other, higher priorities.

In music, drama, and literature, the Nazis were not so tolerant. They did not like the atonality of modern music, and the works of Mendelssohn, Meyerbeer, Mahler, Schoenberg, and other Jewish composers were removed from concert programs. Patriotic songs and Richard Wagner, with his themes of Teutonic superiority, were the preferred genre, although Bach, Beethoven, and Brahms were not completely forgotten. Nor did the Nazis like the expressionist and realistic drama of the Weimar era. Gerhart Hauptmann, the foremost German playwright, accepted the Nazi state, but he had lost his inspiration and produced nothing of value. Most of the other major playwrights left the country, and those who stayed were of lesser quality, concentrating on historical themes but having little of importance to say. The German theater continued to enjoy state subsidies, but most of its successes were classical drama, not new, innovative works.

The same was true in literature. The works of Jews and leftists were banned. When the chamber demanded that writers sign a loyalty oath to the regime and contribute their talents to the party, many left the country. Over 2,000 writers departed between 1933 and 1939, including, among others, Thomas and Heinrich Mann, Kathe Kollwitz, and Richard Huch. Most of those who remained were less than memorable. Hans Grimm wrote, by analogy, of the German need for more Lebensraum, or living space. Erwin Guido Kolbenheyer theorized about subordinating the self to the community. Hanns Johst glorified violence and its importance in establishing the *völkish* German state. Even first-rate writers, like the poets Gottfried Benn and Ernst Jünger, who at first approved of National Socialism, soon became disillusioned and tried to distance themselves from the government. Eventually they went into the military. Benn's and Jünger's difficulties in some ways exemplify the problems of German literature throughout the period, and the lack of vitality or originality in literature can be realized in all areas of higher culture. The Nazi conception of culture was too narrow, too regulated, too antimodern, except perhaps in architecture, to produce any works of lasting value.

In the other main areas under the chamber's jurisdiction—radio, press, and film—the watchwords were propaganda, censorship, and control, along with some entertainment. Propaganda was to present to the people the Nazi version of events, and censorship and control were to ensure that the media did not deviate from that version. In the increasingly popular medium of radio, the state provided both propaganda and entertainment. But the German Information Service, which became part of the government in December 1933, issued the releases that determined the content of all foreign news before its broadcast, and domestic news was also closely monitored.

The same type of thinking applied to newspapers. Anyone associated with the print media had to belong to the Reich Press Chamber. Nazi operatives became the heads of the German associations for publishers and for the press, the publishers under Rolf Rienhardt, the press corps under Otto Dietrich. To make sure that publishers were aware of what the party wanted, the Propaganda Ministry's press agency issued numerous directives at daily news conferences. The party publishing house, Eher Verlag, headed by Max Amann, acquired the ownership—direct or indirect—of most of the country's newspapers. Those that remained independent struggled on, but with restrictions. What this meant, of course, was that the press had lost its independence.

Goebbels was more flexible in his handling of the film industry. In a series of moves between 1933 and 1938, the state took over the entire industry and subjected it to governmental oversight. Goebbels realized, however, that a steady diet of propaganda movies would not be vastly popular, so many of the state-sponsored films were love stories or comedies of the escapist variety. As a result, the number of people attending movies quadrupled between 1938 and 1942. Still the state did sponsor films that highlighted Nazi themes—national unity, leadership, anti-Semitism—though with mixed success. One of the more successful Nazi cinematographers was Leni Riefenstahl. Best known for her "Triumph of the Will," a documentary of the 1934 Nuremberg party rally that made Hitler appear larger than life itself, Riefenstahl became the premier Nazi film director. A person of real talent, she made a number of other movies, including "Olympia" filmed at the 1936 Olympic Games. But Riefenstahl was too temperamental and had difficulty sustaining her early success. Another Nazi director, Karl Ritter, a pilot in World War I, was associated with nationalistic movies that emphasized the heroism of National Socialism in bringing new life to a Germany in despair. Both Ritter and Riefenstahl survived the war, but their close involvement with the Nazis virtually ended their film careers.

In film, as in other areas of culture, the regime was not entirely consistent. The Nazis wanted to infuse culture with their own ideology while ridding it of modernistic influences. Though they had succeeded in removing so-called degenerate art from the galleries, modern designs in furniture and other consumer goods retained their popularity. Modern buildings were not torn down and continued to be used. Until the war began, jazz records remained on sale and were produced in large numbers. Hitler and his followers may have been opposed to modern trends, but these trends were not entirely repressed. Once again the Nazis' inconsistencies in the arts and culture mirrored nearly all aspects of the regime.

WHY NATIONAL SOCIALISM?

Despite having looked at the political, economic, social, and cultural dimensions of nazism, a number of nagging questions still remain. Two of the most important are: What was the appeal of National Socialism?, and Why did the German people succumb to it? While there are no easy answers to these questions, one can point to various possibilities. Though none alone is sufficient, each may provide at least a partial answer. The possibilities, listed in no special order, are as follows:

1) Germany turned to National Socialism because of the depression and the unpopular Weimar government. Economic and political discontent led to Hitler's takeover.

2) The German people approved of the Nazi emphasis on nationalism and militarism. They also agreed with its cultural conservatism, its harsh attitude toward unpopular minorities and deviant groups, and its strict attitude toward youth. The National Socialists thus confirmed and enforced the biases of a substantial portion of the population.

3) National Socialism was something peculiarly German. During the nineteenth century, Germany moved away from the Western humanistic tradition that stressed the rationality and humanity of individuals. Instead, the Bismarckian idea that moral considerations should not govern state actions became the norm in German society. Moreover, German nationalists would not accept the verdict of World War I, and Germany therefore became pitted against democracy. In other words, National Socialism owed a great deal of its success to its German roots.

4) On the other hand, it might be contended that nazism was part of the worldwide upheaval of trying to adapt to the disrup-

tive conditions brought on by industrialization and urbanization. How were countries to cope with these devastating forces? The German solution was National Socialism.

5) Hitler's movement was an outgrowth of Germany's "torn" condition. In the seventeenth and eighteenth centuries, Germany was made up of many religious denominations and many fragmented states. At that time, the German lands were fragmented both religiously and politically, and their leaders did not grapple with the idea of what to do when state authority went wrong. There is a vast difference between dealing with local and national affairs, and there was also the added factor of the Lutheran tradition of obedience, loyalty, and service to the state. Immoral actions in a large state like Germany were something for which the people simply were not ready.

6) The acceptance of National Socialism can be attributed to Hitler. He was not only a bright, charismatic leader with a common touch, he was also a good organizer, who, in effect, was able to make a society go bad. And when an advanced society goes bad, the effects are truly terrible and wide reaching.

7) National Socialism succeeded because German education was too specialized. It produced individuals proficient in special skills or specific knowledge, but it did not educate the whole person. Education was not sufficiently committed to cultivating civil responsibility and ethical standards, and these elements are vital if a humane society is to survive.

8) The Nazi movement took advantage of the division between the educated elite and the slightly educated masses in German society. During the nineteenth century, this became the true dividing line between the ruling oligarchy and its subjects. The subjects sought emancipation from this condition in two ways: the formation of a subculture or a resort to barbarism. The first, the solution of the social democratic movement, was unsuccessful because it was unable to isolate itself or to gain sufficient acceptance from the people. The second was the way of the Nazis. The latter won out. Evidence suggests that Hitler's prestige with the people did not rest exclusively on economic and foreign policy achievements, though they undoubtedly helped. His standing was repeatedly enhanced because he succeeded again and again in defeating and humiliating the members of the old oligarchy.

An additional answer that does not explain the cause for National Socialism's acceptance but helps explain its rapid take-over is the nature of German society itself. By the 1930s, Germany had achieved a high level of technological, educational, and economic prowess. Yet this highly advanced society lapsed into barbarism. A plausible explanation is that the more advanced a society is technologically, and the more complex its structures, the easier the thrust toward barbarism. All of the technological advances—centralization, rapid transportation, mass communications—can readily be used for the thrust downward, and a literate population is also more amenable to change. In short, the higher the level of society, the faster its descent can be. Therefore a high technological level may not be purely positive. And the advanced state of German society was the prime reason for the rapidity of its movement into barbarism. The speed was determined by technology, even though it did not determine the direction. National Socialism well demonstrates that a smart society is not necessarily a good society.

TOWARD WAR

There is now no question that from the time Hitler assumed control of Germany on January 30, 1933, he desired more living space for the privileged Aryan race. It is also now clear that he intended to attain that goal by war. At the time, however, these two cardinal features of Nazi policy were not so obvious. To be sure, observers of the situation soon realized that Hitler's Germany was to be a different Germany and that the country was rearming, a fact that became public knowledge in March 1935, when Hitler renounced the military restrictions in the Versailles treaty and called for a military draft and an independent air force. His aggressive tendencies were also apparent in the summer of 1934. At that time Austrian Nazis had assassinated that nation's chancellor, Engelbert Dollfuss, during an attempted coup, and even though Hitler was not directly involved, he probably knew about it, and he did nothing to prevent it. If Germany had more aggressive designs against its Austrian neighbor, they were restrained when Mussolini placed Italian troops on alert on his northern border to ensure that Hitler did not intervene.

Nevertheless, Hilter's "interest" in Austrian politics was generally the exception to his comportment during the early years, for he did not want to alarm foreign governments—or alienate the populace at home—by moving too fast. Hence, he put up a peaceful front, signing the Concordat with the papacy in July 1933 and a nonaggression pact with Poland, his eastern neighbor, in January 1934. With these agreements, he was able to reinforce the feeling in Britain, France, and other countries that he had become a responsible ruler and that at least some of Germany's international grievances were justified. The Western powers began to wonder why Germany should be saddled with the Versailles restrictions and why German-speaking people who lived outside the Reich should not be allowed to become a part of Germany if they so desired.

Hitler picked up on these themes and used them to great advantage. At this point, Britain and France went along. Not only did they feel a degree of guilt, but they had other reasons for not wanting to become involved militarily against Germany. For one thing, the memories of World War I continued. By the time that conflict had been settled, they had realized that winning had been no better than losing and that another war, in view of the recent technological advances, would be even more horrible.

Moreover, the coalition that had defeated Germany in the last war was no longer intact. Because of the fear of a strong Germany on his northern border, Mussolini might have stayed with the Allies over Austria, but he eventually changed his mind and decided instead to align with Germany. The United States had gone its own way and showed no inclination to shed the blood of its citizens in another European conflict. The Soviet Union, at least for the moment, was also disinterested, since it was pursuing its own policies, including rapid internal industrialization. This lack of powerful allies, along with memories of the last war and the feeling that Germany had been treated unfairly at Versailles, helped set the stage for Britain's and France's reluctance to stand in the way of Germany's clearly aggressive moves during the rest of the 1930s.

Hitler's first overt act in which the Allies might have intervened occurred in March 1936, when he remilitarized the Rhineland, that strip of German land between the Reich and

France and the Low Countries, which was to have been demilitarized in perpetuity as part of the Versailles settlement. But in this instance Hitler was able to take advantage of the confusion in Allied policy toward Italy, which was at the time involved in its own aggression against Ethiopia. The French response, based on its own perceived military weakness and its political instability, was to do nothing (it actually had nothing planned). Britain, which also considered itself unprepared, did not want to become involved either, so Hitler's gamble that the Western governments would not intervene had paid off. As a result, in full defiance of the Versailles treaty, Germany had regained full sovereignty over the Rhineland.

This crisis was an important turning point. Although Britain and France now began considering ways to overcome their military deficiencies, they did nothing to cause Hitler undue alarm. And Italy, increasingly alienated by British and French support of sanctions and other anti-Italian measures during the Ethiopian war, started to move into the Nazi camp, a move consummated with the signing of the Rome-Berlin Axis in August 1936. The Axis had actually already taken tangible shape a month earlier when civil war had broken out in Spain. Italy had responded at once to the Spanish military junta's call for aid by transporting troops and supplies to the battle zone. Germany had been more hesitant but soon followed suit, though on a more limited scale, and it came in on the same side as the Italians. The outcome of Italy's and Germany's involvement was an eventual victory for their Spanish ally, the so-called Nationalists, led by General Francisco Franco.

The Rhineland remilitarization also had another repercussion. Now that Hitler's western boundary problem had been solved, he felt he could take further initiatives. He planned to build up Germany's defenses in the west so that he could keep Britain and France from intervening, while he concentrated on central and eastern Europe. During 1937, Hitler began construction of a series of western fortifications, and he bided his time. But in November, he called together his top military leaders and ministers and told them of his next projected moves. Germany, he said, had to solve its need for more land forthwith, and Austria and Czechoslovakia were to be its first victims.

Three months later, in February 1938, he began to carry out his plans. On the 4th, he met the young Austrian chancellor, Kurt von Schuschnigg, and demanded that he make numerous concessions, including amnesty to those imprisoned for their involvement in the assassination of former Chancellor Dollfuss, the placement of Austrian Nazis into key positions in Schuschnigg's cabinet, and the appointment of German military advisers to serve in the Austrian army. If Schuschnigg did not agree to these demands, Hitler threatened the German invasion of Austria.

What followed for Schuschnigg was a month of frenzied diplomatic activity (Britain and France expressed grave concern, but little else), numerous political moves and countermoves inside Austria, and unremitting German pressure. In the end, he gave in and resigned; an Austrian Nazi leader, Artur Seyss-Inquart, was named in his place, and on March 12, German troops marched across the border into Austria. There was no resistance, and Austria soon became part of the new Greater German Reich. The Führer could not have been more pleased.

As Hitler had indicated the previous November, Czechoslovakia was to become Germany's next center of conflict. He was convinced that Czechoslovakia would have to be absorbed through war. He and his military advisers believed they could win a war against the Czechs and Slovaks, but they knew that they had to win it quickly and visibly so that no outside power would be inclined to intervene. However, their desire for a localized war presented a problem, for there was a possibility that the war might not be so rapid—the Czechs were fairly well defended—and an extended conflict would give Britain and France an opportunity to come in on the Czechoslovak side and therefore bring about an enlarged, two-front war.

This problem prompted Hitler to try to isolate Czechoslovakia from its Western supporters by putting the Czechs in the wrong. For this purpose, he decided to use the Sudeten Germans, three million Germans who had lived in western Czechoslovakia for centuries and who had a small Nazi party. He claimed that these Sudeten Germans, most of whom lived near the German border, were being oppressed and should be allowed to become a part of Germany if that was their wish. This was a good argument for allowing Hitler to localize the war, for Britain and France concluded that even if they went to war and won, based on the principle of self-determination, they would have to cede the Sudeten area to Germany anyway. They were thus willing to give up the Sudetenland to save part of Czechoslovakia, and, more important from their point of view, to sacrifice the area in order to avoid war. Needless to say, the Czechoslovak government would have been appalled had they known what the British and French were thinking.

The Germans began their "campaign" in May 1938 by instigating a flare-up along the Czech border and by instructing the Sudeten Nazis to foment discontent within the country. The situation, accompanied by a flurry of diplomatic activity, quieted down over the summer, but Hitler was again sabre rattling in September. This time the British, led by Neville Chamberlain, and the French, with the Italians acting as a go-between, met with Hitler in a series of meetings to try to iron out their differences. The Czechs were not invited to attend the meeting, and the Soviets, who by now were quite interested in what was going on in the region, were also kept on the sidelines. Chamberlain and Hitler did not really want to listen to the other parties anyway, and they relegated to themselves the key decisions. At their last meeting on September 29, the British prime minister went to Munich and with the French premier, Eduard Daladier, and Mussolini joining in the discussions, the Western powers acceded in general to Hitler's demands that the Sudeten area come under German domination. War had thus been averted at Munich, and the British and French populace were overjoyed: the Sudetenland had been the price, but from the Western standpoint, the price had been well worth it.

The elation in Britain and France was short-lived, however, for Hitler now decided to go even further. In fact, he was infuriated after Munich because he had only received what he asked for, not what he had truly wanted—all of Czechoslovakia. Chamberlain and Daladier had deprived him of his little war. Now he had to take more time to gain control of the entire country. Fortunately for him, two of Czechoslovakia's neighbors, Poland and Hungary, also had claims to Czech and Slovak territory, and in November, he awarded them each small portions, a measure that kept them in line when, on March 15, 1939, he took over the Czech half of the country and established a protectorate over the Slovak half. In effect, Czechoslovakia was no more, and its resources, as pointed out earlier, could now be put to use as part of the German war machine.

This latest action provoked a violent reaction inside Britain and France. Chamberlain had had Hitler's word at Munich that he had no further territorial ambitions: he had broken his promise and obviously could no longer be trusted. Just as obviously, Hitler had not been satisfied with taking the German-speaking areas like the Sudetenland. He must have other, bigger goals in mind, and, they felt, his next act of aggression had to be resisted. Even if the Western governments wavered in their resolve, public opinion in Britain and France would not stand for any more Munichs.

Hitler, on the other hand, had concluded that the Western powers might not have the will, perhaps ever, to fight, over eastern Europe. If this were indeed the case, so much the better. If not, he would have to take them on sooner or later anyway, and it might as well be now. In other words, he was willing to take his chances.

For awhile, Hitler contemplated attacking either west or east, but during April 1939, he decided to move east against Poland. He again manufactured an issue—guaranteed access through Poland's Danzig corridor that separated East Prussia from the rest of Germany—and again he attempted to drive a diplomatic wedge, this time between Poland and its Western partners by courting the Soviet Union. Hitler eventually succeeded in bringing the Soviets around by offering them concessions of land in eastern Europe, concessions that the British and French, who were also negotiating with the Russians, were unwilling to make. On August 23, he announced to the world that Germany and the Soviet Union had signed a non-aggression pact. Even though they kept secret those articles that divided large portions of eastern Europe into German and Soviet "spheres of influence," Hitler expected that his diplomatic coup might well detach Britain and France from their Polish ally, since they presumed that help would come from the Soviets in case war broke out over Poland.

But Britain and France did not abandon Poland. Instead, they reaffirmed their commitment to the Poles, and they also pressured Germany's Italian ally to indicate to Hitler their determination. As a result of these initiatives, Hitler decided to postpone the attack—it now was set for August 26—to give one last try to drive Poland and Britain and France apart. When negotiations broke down, he did allow Italy to opt out at least for the time being, but he still resolved to go to war. On the night of August 31, he had an incident staged near the German-Polish border, and the next morning German forces started streaming into Poland. Britain and France issued warnings to the Germans to cease and desist. When they did not, the six long years of World War II began.

5 / GERMANY DURING
THE WAR, 1939–1945

Not surprisingly, the war on the battle fronts dominated the thinking and actions of the German public at home. But what happened on the home front was also exceedingly important, for total warfare in the twentieth century does not allow military forces to live primarily off the land: it requires the combatants to depend also on their people and the products they manufacture to sustain the war effort. In this context, the Nazi government, though authoritarian, was concerned about the people's morale and their response to the conflict. It was further concerned about having a strong economy at home as well as being able to use additional resources from abroad, gained through conquest or from pressure on countries nearby, and these activities helped determine the course of the war.

This was also a time during which other drastic changes occurred. The Nazis began to treat the Jews even more horribly than they had before, and the mass executions in which they engaged are almost too horrible to contemplate. While many Germans and the people living in the occupied areas and in the satellite states had only a vague idea of the atrocities that the Nazis were actually performing, some individuals and small groups became so disillusioned with what was happening to the Jews, or with other Nazi policies, that they desired to overthrow the regime. Their lack of numbers and cohesion, however, spelled the ultimate failure of the various resistance groups inside Germany. Their failures, along with the people's reaction to the war, the war economy, and the treatment of the Jews, provide additional insights into wartime Germany besides those gleaned from the battlefronts.

THE PEOPLE'S RESPONSE

The interaction between propaganda and public opinion determined people's response to the conflict. The state, through Goebbels's Propaganda Ministry, controlled the media and tried to use them to manipulate public opinion. But Goebbels and Hitler were well aware that manipulation had its limits. Their propaganda had to be believable, so the SD, after sampling the public mood, issued weekly reports, and other agencies also attempted to get an idea of what the public was thinking. The primary Nazi goal, of course, was to paint as positive a picture as possible of the war in order to sustain the public's morale. They did not exclude lying, but even lies had to be credible. It was not too difficult for the government to report a rosy scenario as long as the war was going well for them, but when it began to go badly, as it did increasingly after late 1941, and especially after the disaster at Stalingrad a year later, the propaganda machine faced its greatest challenge—to paint black as white. In the end, German propaganda did not succeed, but it probably did about as well as could have been expected, especially given the massive destruction and losses that the war entailed for Germany.

At least part of the reason for the success of Goebbels's propaganda program was his attempt, through the reports his ministry received, to be sensitive to public opinion. Another part of the reason was that he and his cohorts took advantage of the various popular stereotypes and objectives held by many persons in German society. The elite was quite agreeable to Nazi political goals, as long as the full extent of these goals was not public knowledge. The government also realized that the churches would be a focal point for the populace during times of trial and concern, and thus, at least for a while, muted their persecution of them. Working- and middle-class support were vital, and propaganda officials therefore took great care not to alienate them if possible. Since women and youth remained largely apolitical, the propaganda machine did not accord them special concern, except later in the war when they deemed their participation in the war effort to be crucial.

The Nazis further realized that the public was susceptible to foreign national stereotypes, which changed as the course of the war changed. The ministry therefore tried to portray the Japanese positively, since they were an ally, but it could barely hide its contempt for the Italians, whom the Germans had never held in high esteem. The view that propaganda officials took toward the French altered from negative to positive after France's defeat in 1940, but it again became negative once pro-Allied sentiments had become evident among the French populace. Among the Allies, the ministry depicted the British and later the Americans in less than flattering terms, and once Germany turned against the Soviet Union in mid-1941, its propaganda kept up an unremitting torrent of anti-Bolshevik, anti-Jewish, and anti-Semitic rhetoric. There were instances, however, when Goebbels may have gone too far. Despite the onslaught of propaganda, some Germans started to display a grudging respect for the resolution of the British and the Americans. Even toward the Soviets, the public image changed to an extent when ordinary Germans found the eastern laborers among them to be intelligent and likable, even though this view changed dramatically when the Red Army began to sweep across Germany.

As before the war, the population seldom exhibited prowar tendencies even during the conflict. At first, at the outbreak of the war against Poland on September 1, 1939, the public mood was one of stolid resignation. There was little evidence of war fever, but little opposition either. The stock market declined, the regime forbade the people under the threat of punishment to listen to foreign radio broadcasts, and they also imposed wartime measures, such as additional food rationing and higher taxes. The ministry spent part of its time denying rumors of military setbacks, excessive troop losses, and acts of sabotage to reassure the populace that all was going well, and they also countered stories of German atrocities in Poland by emphasizing that ethnic Germans were being murdered by Poles and that subjects of the British Empire were being tortured by their colonial masters. Still, the basic German attitude was one of unenthusiastic acceptance. After Poland fell within a month, the people's outlook improved, particularly when Hitler's speech on October 6 contained a proposal for peace with the Western powers, which reawakened hopes for a quick end to the war.

But, of course, the war did not end. The Soviet Union had signed a non-aggression pact with the government before the

Polish campaign and thus was not an enemy, though it had taken over the eastern portion of Poland as part of its price for not standing in the way of the German aggression. The main opponents, Britain and France, had declared war, but had undertaken only minor offensive actions, so the antagonists settled back into what has been called the Phony War, or as the Germans described it, the *Sitzkrieg*, or "sitting war." During this time, the fall and winter of 1939–40, the German public became aware of a deterioration in its hardly extravagant standard of living, and people started complaining about inadequate food rations. They also voiced complaints about a lack of leather shoes and insufficient allotments of coal. The lack of coal became so acute that in several instances police had to be called in to quell angry crowds who were threatening various retail coal dealers. There was further open discontent from the clergy, Communist groups, and students, the latter in terms of their lack of enthusiasm for the military cause. However, cases of outright defiance were relatively rare during what was mostly a period of austerity and boredom.

The German military attacks on Norway and Denmark in April 1940 and on France and the Low Countries in May actually produced an upsurge of morale, and rapid victories in both campaigns were considered great triumphs for the regime. The people's elation was partly related to the hope that France's defeat in June might mean an end to the conflict, since Britain, too, might agree to a peace settlement rather than face a German invasion. But when Britain rejected Hitler's peace overtures in July, the people realized that they were in for more fighting. By now, however, they revered Hitler as a hero, and the victory celebration in Berlin in July was the high point of support for the government.

The public was also generally supportive of the late summer air offensive against Britain, but when the Luftwaffe failed to drive the Royal Air Force from the skies and Hitler called off the invasion of the British Isles, a type of national listlessness set in. Workers complained about fixed wages, the rising costs of living, and the poor quality of food, especially sausage and cheese. Large numbers of Germans criticized the government for the monotony of the news they were receiving. The government further worried about the attitude of the people as the second wartime winter, with its attendant shortages, approached. Yet on the whole, the people were more war weary than opposed to the regime. The Führer's prestige was higher than ever, and hardly anyone doubted an eventual German victory.

Meanwhile, the Wehrmacht planned additional conquests. The public hailed the swift operations against Yugoslavia and Greece in the spring of 1941, but the German offensive against its supposed ally, the USSR, on June 22, opened a new phase of the war. Initially, the invasion of Russia shocked the German people, but amidst the flood of anti-Soviet propaganda and depictions of Russian war atrocities, most Germans soon became reconciled to the eastern campaign. Although government propaganda reported a series of stunning victories, not always accurately, the mood of the population fluctuated. They were still quite anxious about food scarcities, and church leaders began to speak out against Nazi policies, particularly concerning the euthanasia program, which Hitler officially halted in August 1941. By September, letters from soldiers at the front indicated the real difficulties they faced, such as a lack of ammunition and provisions and a seemingly endless supply of Red Army reserves. That same month, the government ordered all Jews to wear a yellow Star of David on their outer clothing. Most Germans greeted this new regulation favorably or apathetically, but a few persons did try to help their Jewish acquaintances as the number of anti-Semitic measures multiplied. In October, when the Wehrmacht launched an attack against Moscow, designed to bring the eastern campaign to a swift conclusion, Hitler declared the war all but won.

But, as in previous years, the war was not over. The Soviet Union did not fold, and, in fact, it launched a counteroffensive in early December. At nearly the same time, Japan bombed Pearl Harbor and brought a previously hesitant United States into the conflict. Germany stood by its Japanese ally by declaring war on the United States, so by the end of 1941, the two alliances were in place. The main Axis powers consisted of Germany, Japan, and Italy, the Allied coalition of Great Britain, the Soviet Union, and the United States.

During the winter of 1941–42, the German public was increasingly disgruntled. The deteriorating military situation and the length of the war were taking its toll. There was unrest among youth, mounting criticisms of the government's unrealistic propaganda, and growing dissatisfaction even among the Nazi faithful. On the other hand, the people were indicating increasing mistrust of party officials, not of Hitler himself. More and more letters from the fronts were relating the hardships there—cold, sickness, poor food. At home, the government announced a further reduction in food rations on February 3. Allied bombing—on Lübeck in March, Augsburg in April, and Cologne, Essen, and Bremen in May and June—brought damage to those cities and apprehension throughout the Reich.

At midyear, the military situation brightened with successful operations in southern portions of the Soviet Union and against the British in North Africa, but during the fall, difficulties again set in. The British drove back Axis troops from El Alamein in Egypt, and a combined Anglo-American landing in Northwest Africa succeeded and began moving east. Even more devastating was the German setback at Stalingrad, where the Red Army surrounded Axis formations in November 1942 and forced them to surrender the following February. The initiative had definitely turned in favor of the Allies.

The Stalingrad defeat actually spurred the Propaganda Ministry to even greater efforts. Near the end of the battle, Goebbels read a speech, commemorating the tenth anniversary of the Nazi takeover, in which he proclaimed a new strategy: total war. He followed this with another total war speech on February 18 before a huge crowd at the Berlin Sports Palace. After haranguing the crowd to a frenzied pitch, heightened by taped applause played over the loudspeaker system, he asked a series of questions: Are you ready to do battle? Are you resolved to work harder? Are you willing to undertake total war? Are you demonstrating absolute faith in the Führer? As one might expect, the response in each instance was a resounding yes.

While the government succeeded in avoiding any demonstrations after the defeat at Stalingrad, it could not avoid noticing signs of discontent. Reports from the fronts of "flexible defense and well-planned withdrawals" caused alarm. Even censored letters from the soldiers could not cover up stories of intolerable conditions on the battlefronts in Russia and Tunisia. There was also growing unrest among the civil service because policies were not being implemented effectively. Laborers, many of

whom worked ten-to-twelve-hour shifts, were reportedly express-
ing a preference for communism over nazism. The growing
numbers of foreign workers in the country were forcing the
Gestapo to spend increasing amounts of its time policing them,
especially since the domestic work force was becoming more and
more reluctant to inform on their foreign coworkers.

From mid-1943 to mid-1944, the turns the war was taking only
reinforced the gloomy atmosphere at home. By early summer,
the German submarine force, which had caused the British,
Canadians, and Americans untold difficulties earlier in the war,
had been virtually driven from the Atlantic. After clearing North
Africa, the Western allies invaded Sicily in July and began to move
up the peninsula in September. During these same months,
Mussolini's own party overthrew him, and the new Italian government opted out of the war. These moves spelled additional
burdens from the Wehrmacht's attempt to defend southern
Europe. After the Soviets turned back the Germans in a massive tank battle around Kursk on the eastern front, their retreat
out of Russia continued apace. Those on leave brought home
increasingly pessimistic reports. Soldiers on all fronts were show-
ing signs of defeatism. The least-interested and most indifferent segment of the home front population were the women. Only
those women with family on the battlefronts followed the military
happenings, and only then in those sectors where the family
member or members were deployed. Marriages began to suffer
from long separations, and more and more people became involved in extramarital affairs. The widespread evacuation of
women and children from endangered zones caused further
strains on family life. Also, by this time, Allied bombing raids
were exacting a heavy price on Hamburg, Berlin, and other cities
throughout the Reich, and by the beginning of 1944, fears of
a US-British invasion from the west were mounting.

The Allied D-day assault of the Normandy coast on June 6,
1944, ushered in the final stage of the war. It was horrible for
Germans at the fronts and at home. The German response to
the D-day invasion had been the launching of V-weapons, some
of Hitler's arsenal of so-called "miracle weapons," against targets in Britain. But besides giving the Germans a temporary lift,
these unmanned bombs (and later rockets) proved to be more
psychologically than physically damaging, for they resulted in

only moderate destruction at best. More significantly, the Wehrmacht was losing territory in the west, British and American forces had taken Rome and were racing northward in Italy, and the Soviets unleashed a powerful offensive in the east. Topping all of these disastrous developments was an attempt on Hitler's life. On July 20th, a group of army officers planted a bomb in his headquarters during a briefing. It had gone off, and though it killed several of the military officers in attendance, the Führer was only slightly injured. The assassination attempt actually helped the sagging prestige of the regime, at least for a while, since the disloyal conduct of the July 20th "criminals," shocked and offended most Germans.

By late summer, however, except for a small minority, few Germans still believed that victory was possible. The enemy was approaching German soil from both the east and the west. The government ordered all males between the ages of fifteen and sixty-five, who were not already in the armed forces, to serve in either construction units or home guard formations, and some women joined the final effort as well. But the people greeted radio and newspaper propaganda with growing disbelief, and one remark heard with increasing frequency was as follows: "The claim is always made that the Führer was sent to us by God. I don't doubt it. The Führer was sent by God, not to save Germany, but rather to ruin her."[1] A German offensive through the Ardennes forest, the aptly named Battle of the Bulge, gave rise to some optimism over Christmas 1944. But the Americans soon closed the gap, and the Soviets undertook another offensive just after the first of the year with devastating results.

By 1945, with the end of the war near, most Germans awaited their fate. Despite the increased privations and widespread dislocations, the party continued to try to shore up the people's morale. It held mass funerals and memorial services for soldiers of the Reich throughout the country. The film "Kolberg," in which the heroic inhabitants of Kolberg gather in their city to celebrate their willingness to die so that the nation might live and experience a rebirth, was a technicolor production shown in numerous movie theaters. As a fitting, final tribute, the Berlin

---

1 Marlis Steinert, *Hitler's War and the Germans: Public Mood and Attitude during the Second World War* (Athens, Ohio, 1977), 284.

Philharmonic at its last concert played Wagner's "Twilight of the Gods," which depicts the destruction of the legendary Valhalla and the end of the world.

The German government played out the last months in what today seems a surrealistic finale. By all rights, it should have sued for peace, but as long as Hitler was in control, he would not hear of surrender. He had decided that the German people were not worthy of him. If they were defeated, it had shown that they were not superior. He therefore identified the fate of the German people with his own fate. If he lost, they should lose also. If he were killed, they, too, should perish.

During these last hectic days in his underground headquarters in Berlin, Hitler determined to take his own life. On April 29, 1945, with the Red Army closing in, he married Eva Braun and dictated his last will and testament. In it, he denied wanting to start the war, claiming that it had been part of a Jewish plot; expelled Göring and Himmler from the party, since they had been negotiating with the Allies behind his back; appointed his successors; explained his recent marriage; disposed of his property; and announced his impending death. On the 30th, he arose around noon and ate a light lunch. He and his new wife then retired to their quarters. When his entourage entered the rooms about an hour later, they realized that the two of them had taken poison and that Hitler had also shot himself. They took the bodies upstairs, out of the underground bunker, and burned them in a nearby bomb crater. The next day, Red Army soldiers found the remains of the bodies, although this information was not known for certain in the West for some years after the war, since the Soviets refused to give British and U.S. authorities conclusive proof of the deaths. Also, on May 1, Soviet troops had found in the bunker the bodies of Goebbels, his wife, and their six children. Like their Führer, they had also committed suicide.

Hitler's successor, Grand Admiral Karl Dönitz, was more realistic. He soon contacted the Western allied field commanders, and the Germans surrendered on May 8, 1945, V-E Day, the day of Allied victory in Europe. The Third Reich had come to an end.

Nevertheless, Hitler's appeal among the German people had held almost to the last. The propaganda machine had played a significant role in sustaining his positive image. As the war lengthened, criticisms of the regime had mounted, but seldom were they levelled against the Führer. He was almost above criticism. The myth of him as a thoughtful, resolute, dynamic leader, developed in the 1930s, had carried over to make him a hero during the war itself. The blind faith with which many Germans had accepted Hitler has caused some of them great anguish ever since.

THE WAR ECONOMY

The nature of Germany's war economy, especially during the early years of the conflict, has been a subject of considerable historical debate. The orthodox view for some time had been that the German state, while geared toward war, did not institute a full war economy until late 1941–42. The reason being that between 1939 and 1941, Germany overcame its opponents in a series of short, one-front wars that did not require a total war economy. *Blitzkrieg*, or lightning war, necessitated only a *Blitzkrieg*, or short war economy to sustain it. These wars did not require large stockpiles of arms and ammunition, only enough to prepare for the next victim, and civilian consumption, though reduced during these conflicts, did not have to be cut as drastically as it would have had the fighting been extended. However, once the Germans did indeed become bogged down in a long, protracted conflict against the Soviet Union, the nature of the war changed, forcing Germany to move to a total war economy.

For many historians, the idea of a Blitzkrieg economy is becoming less and less acceptable. While not denying that Germany did not move to a full war economy as soon as some of the other combatants, such as Great Britain, they do not see Blitzkrieg warfare as the main determinant. Instead they cite the very nature of the German economy itself. In their view, Germany did not fully mobilize early on because of poor planning, structural constraints within German industry, and jurisdictional disputes that hindered policy implementation. They relate faulty planning to Hitler's long-term armaments-building program, which he proclaimed at the beginning of 1939. The war had broken out at the program's inception, not at its completion, which had been projected for around 1944. And initially the Wehrmacht did not need battleships or four-engined bombers, but other types of weapons, such as tactical bombers and tanks.

Moreover, although portions of German industry did not oppose a full war economy, they did not actually move in that direction as rapidly or as inexpensively as Hitler would have liked. German industry traditionally had a preference for well-made goods, produced on a small-scale, for which prices were high. To move toward mass production, while maintaining quality, would take time. Also, before the war broke out, some portions of industry managed to resist the government's wishes to an extent, for they expected to benefit from the booming economy by producing more consumer items instead of military hardware. In addition, the government had to build up the military infrastructure—barracks, airfields, etc.—and this, too, required time. As for the jurisdictional conflicts, at first, central planning was woefully inadequate. The armed forces had a number of procurement offices, the Four-Year Plan had its own divisions, the party agencies had their priorities, and the Labor and Economics ministries also had at least some involvement in the economic decision making. As a consequence, policies remained in a muddle for several years into the war.

During the war, then, three principle things shaped the German economy. The amount of the economy devoted to civilian production and consumption decreased. In terms of car production, for instance, the number declined from 276,592 in 1938 to 35,194 in 1941, and the number of housing units from approximately 330,000 to 80,000 during the same period. Civilians also experienced shortages in heating fuel and clothing, and their diet began to consist more and more of ersatz, or substitute, foods, such as gravy tablets and turnip bread. At the same time, the proportion of the economy devoted to military spending increased, but at a relatively slow and consistent rate. In 1938–39, military expenditures made up about made up about 17.6 percent of the total national income; in 1939–40, it was 34.9 percent; in 1940–41, 46.6 percent; and in 1941–42, 57.8 percent. Obviously, these figures do not support a dramatic jump in production.

Finally, a more national wartime economy began to gel as the first step toward centralization took place in March 1940, when Hitler appointed Fritz Todt, the builder of the autobahns and a Four-Year–Plan official, to head the Ministry for Armaments and Munitions. From this new position, Todt sought to streamline procurement and production by reorganizing the entire armaments system. Although often frustrated by the multiplicity of military and civilian agencies involved, he did make some headway.

When Todt was killed in an airplane crash in February 1942, he was succeeded by the ambitious and energetic Albert Speer. Although a surprise choice, Speer continued the work Todt had begun. He developed a system known as "organized improvisation," which he acknowledged having borrowed from Walter Rathenau, who had instituted it during World War I. (It had been used to an extent by Todt earlier.) It involved bringing military and civilian personnel together into branch committees to plan and develop the various types of weapons needed by the military services, supervise and speed up weapons production, and suggest improvements in manufacturing techniques and distribution. These committees ultimately went so far as to handle the transfer of skilled labor between factories when necessary and to undertake investments in buildings and equipment. Still, Speer, whose ministry's name was changed in September 1943 to the more appropriate Ministry for Armaments and War Production, did not rule with a heavy hand. He set up a steering committee to coordinate the activities of the ministry's various branches but let the committees themselves direct and execute their respective responsibilities.

Speer did exhibit a heavy handedness, however, when it came to consolidation. Through a combination of pressure and persistence, he was eventually able to overcome most of the competing groups. First the army in 1942, then the navy and the other economic sectors in 1943, and finally the air force by mid-1944 were brought under his control. Only the SS economic enterprises, the chemical industry, and labor procurement remained outside his direct purview.

Speer's rise to prominence also represented a shift in power among the Nazi leadership. After 1941, Göring's role was diminishing. Even though he still headed the Four-Year Plan, it was becoming little more than a number of individual organizations that competed among themselves and exercised little authority. Besides Speer, real power was being exerted by Himmler, Goebbels, and Bormann. These men were now the powers behind the dictatorship.

The results Speer achieved were impressive. Between 1941 and mid-1944, monthly ammunition production went up 3½ times, tank production 6 times, aircraft production 3 times. During the same period, the proportion of weapons and ammunition being produced rose from 16 to 40 percent of the Nazis' overall industrial output, while that devoted to construction work dropped from 13 to 6 percent and consumer goods from 28 to 22 percent. By 1943–44, direct and indirect expenditures for military related items amounted to an astounding 76.5 percent of the national income.

The government financed the war through various means—taxes, loans, expanding the money supply, exploiting the occupied territories. Taxes were increased only slightly above prewar levels but still made up about one-third of the state's income. Another third came from short-term Reich securities, such as treasury bills, and a fifth came from medium- and long-term loans, which institutional investors, such as banks and insurance companies, were required to finance. The remaining approximate one-eighth of Germany's income was derived from the occupied areas and from private domestic war contributions. The result was widespread inflation and huge debts, which became all too evident after the war was over.

Obviously, the entire economy had been skewed toward the war effort. The Labor Front's "Strength through Joy" organization set up recreation areas for the soldiers and sponsored live entertainment for them in the war zones. The party's vast welfare agency helped resettle racial Germans, evacuated civilians from urban to rural areas, aided air raid victims, and ran the Winter Help program. Many older persons volunteered to serve as air raid wardens and to assist with civil defense matters. Still, there were privations. The average daily caloric intake for Germans declined only slightly, from 2,400 calories in 1941 to 2,000 in early 1945, though the daily intake was much less for foreign workers and concentration camp prisoners. Still the diet for most Germans deteriorated, and by mid-1944, Allied bombing was forcing numerous families from their homes, and the transportation system was becoming a shambles. War industry was also being effected, as a number of industries decentralized their operations.

As for individual industries, they form a great contrast. One that did exceedingly well was the chemical industry dominated by I.G. Farben. Farben became an almost unbelievable conglomerate that manufactured a diverse range of products from pharmaceuticals, dyes, and photographic materials to explosives and synthetic fuel and rubber. It had 334 plants, including a number at Auschwitz, and at its peak employed 330,000 workers. It had problems similar to those of other firms—labor shortages brought on by the war, difficulties getting raw materials and parts, increasing dependence on the state's war policies. But Farben went farther than other companies. It seemingly embraced National Socialism to the fullest extent. The reasons Farben became so enmeshed with nazism are many and varied. As noted, Nazi economic policy was based on the premise that businesses should still be allowed to make a profit, and the result was that Farben let itself be manipulated as to how it made its money. The firm also feared it would be cut out by competitors, especially when the SS assumed a more prominent position in the economy. Patriotism among its executives further played a role, as did the demands for efficiency and the desire for success. Farben did not necessarily condone what the Nazis were doing to the Jews, but they turned a blind eye to it and even contracted many Jewish concentration camp laborers for their factories. Ambition, achievement, tolerance, and collaboration were all factors in what can only be described as a "sell-out" to the regime.

An industry with a different outcome was the coal industry, centered in the Ruhr region. It became caught up in the war, as did the other industries, but it never developed a close relationship with the regime. Its main problem was that it simply could not produce enough coal. The takeover of Polish mines and tighter controls over consumption provided temporary relief, but the industry was still unable to maintain prewar output levels, particularly because of a shortage of labor, though a large-scale influx of foreign workers helped. By mid-1943, productivity was hurt further by Allied air raids, and by early 1944, a breakdown in transportation had replaced production as the biggest bottleneck in the coal supply problem. The government eventually talked the coal companies into setting up a nationwide consortium to cut down on competition and to create savings in distribution, but the measures were too late to have much of an effect. In spite of governmental concern, the coal industry's reticence to accept outside criticism, its lack of dynamism—it never developed any significant technological breakthroughs—and its unimpressive growth prevented it from ever becoming a Nazi industrial favorite.

In agriculture, the problem of insufficient numbers of workers was also prevalent, as was a lack of farm machinery brought on by the manufacturers' priorities to produce armaments. However, the use of conscripted and foreign laborers and foodstuffs from the occupied areas helped offset the agricultural sector's difficulties. The farming community was further assisted by its long-time relationship with the government. This relationship had been usurped by the Four-Year Plan in the late 1930s, but at the outbreak of the war, the Food Estate was placed directly under Darré's Ministry of Food and Agriculture, and the government virtually took over agriculture. Darré proved less than effective as an administrator, so he was shoved aside and eventually replaced by his longtime deputy, Herbert Backe, in 1942. The government worked down to the regional and local levels, directing the food-rationing program, overseeing production and distribution, and determining the amount of food farmers were allowed to keep. As a result of these policies, the German population remained reasonably well fed until toward war's end. Through rationing, the population had sufficient grain, potatoes, and sugar beets, though they still lacked fats. Farmers did produce some vegetable oils, but not enough, and they were still hurt by insufficient fertilizers for crops and a shortage of fodder for their livestock.

An often overlooked aspect of the National Socialist economy was the part played by the SS. During the war, Himmler amassed more and more power, so that he eventually oversaw not only concentration camps, the police, and state security, but also other areas, such as the Interior Ministry and various aspects of the military—from intelligence to reserve forces to the actual command of combat troops. Even before the war, he had begun to move into the economic arena, and this move accelerated during the conflict. By late in the war, the SS operated 150 businesses that were involved in all types of production, such as mining, the manufacture of special armaments, and the extraction of mineral water. Except for a small number of engineers, most of the workers were forced labor, including inmates from the concentration camps. The largest of the firms, the German Earth and Stoneworks Company, began primarily as a construction company but ultimately switched to the production of weapons and ammunition. Toward the end, the SS also built aircraft for the Messerschmitt company in underground shelters inside its concentration camps. And if there was one area of the economy in which the term "slave labor" was applicable, it was the SS enterprises.

Obviously, all sectors of the economy had difficulties securing sufficient workers. In March 1942, Hitler finally tried to resolve the issue by appointing Fritz Sauckel, the Gau leader of Thuringia, to an additional new post, General Plenipotentiary for the Allocation of Labor. While nominally under the Four-Year Plan, in reality Sauckel and his agency were given almost unlimited authority to secure workers. Though resisted by others, especially Speer, who contended that foreign laborers would be more productive if they remained in their own countries, Sauckel ruthlessly combed the occupied territories for workers to make up for the deficiencies in the Reich.

A look at the employment figures provides an idea of the extent to which Sauckel succeeded. During the conflict, the civilian labor force stabilized at about 36 million. While the number of males in the work force decreased from 24.4 million in May 1939 to 13.5 million in September 1944, the total number of females remained relatively constant, from 14.6 million to 14.9 million, during the same period. Thus, in September 1944, the number of women surpassed that of men in the work force. The remaining shortage was shored up by foreign and forced labor. Concentration camp prisoners and prisoners of war provided some of the difference, but most of the workers were brought in from outside the Reich. Their total increased from 301,000, or .8 percent, of the work force in May 1939, to 7,500,000, or 20.8 percent, in September 1944. In all, approximately 12 million foreign laborers worked in Germany during the war.

The conditions under which most foreign laborers worked varied from tolerable to horrible. An example of their appalling living conditions was experienced by many who worked in the mines. Miners lived in overcrowded, wooden barracks without electricity, running water, or surfaced floors. Wool blankets were not provided. Toilet facilities consisted of trenches, the smell of which was only made more unbearable by the spray used as a disinfectant. Discipline was strictly enforced, and the laborers were subject to long hours of work, mostly underground, and were often punished if they could not keep up with their quotas. Unproductive workers—the sick and the pregnant women—were sent away, but since some of the living areas had minimal or no medical treatment available, many who left work never returned. The Welfare Agency was often responsible for the pregnant women. At first, mothers and their babies were sent back to their home countries as a cost-saving move, though the mother was often required to return. After 1942, the agency established child collection points, at which newborns were handled according to racial selection procedures. Those babies considered especially "valuable" were turned over to the SS Lebensborn organization. Those considered "totally unacceptable" racially were starved to death in "care centers," their corpses packed into cardboard boxes and incinerated.

Yet, in spite of the horrors, there were some ameliorating factors. As mentioned, the attitude of Germans, particularly fellow workers, toward the foreign laborers began to change. It was realized that they were vital to the war effort, and the officials in charge of the foreign laborers were concerned about raising worker productivity. They therefore instituted training programs and, at times, provided even the foreign workers with recreational facilities. Their wages, though still low, were increased, so on occasion were their food rations, and special rewards were sometimes meted out to those who surpassed quotas. Still, behind every incentive was an implied threat of force. Food rations could be used as a punishment as well as an incentive. Workers could be beaten as well as rewarded. By late 1943–44, the attitudes of the foreign workers worsened. Cases of absenteeism and feigned illnesses to avoid work rose. Factory guards responded by turning some recalcitrant laborers over to the SS, who then sent them to work in concentration camps. Nevertheless, the foreign workers remained relatively docile. They instigated a mutiny at Hamburg in the summer of 1943, but it was promptly put down, and some laborers joined a resistance group in Cologne in late 1944. But these instances were exceptions. Overall, the foreigners worked hard and provided the Nazis with a valuable, cheap source of labor.

Foreign workers, of course, were only part of the value that the Nazis reaped from occupied Europe. That the Nazis did not take better advantage of the occupied areas, however, was one of their most telling failures. Hitler and his minions looked upon them merely as regions to be exploited to the fullest. They might eventually be integrated into an economic whole, but that would have to wait. Politically, the Nazis did not, for the most part, do away with the existing nation-state system of the occupied territories. Only those areas closest to Germany, such as Alsace-Lorraine and western Poland, were incorporated into the Greater German Reich. Most of the other areas were either administered directly by German military or civilian officials, as in the case of the Netherlands, Belgium, central Poland, and the western Soviet Union, or became satellites, as in the case of Slovakia, Hungary, Romania, and Vichy France (until November 1942). As part of Hitler's New Order, these areas were accorded varying degrees of sovereignty, but the immediate Nazi goal was to use them to help Germany fight its war. Their treatment followed a type of pattern. As the war continued, German pressure on them mounted, economic demands were raised, and forced deportations, especially of Jews and workers, were exacted. Local officials were forced to make more and more concessions, which provoked increasing resentment among the populaces, and which, in turn, led to organized resistance throughout occupied Europe.

Particularly resented was the Nazis' blatant economic exploitation. The citizenry of the respective areas was obliged to pay
the costs of living of their German occupiers, which were set far
in excess to the actual costs, and the German currency, the
Reichsmark, was pegged at an artificially high rate in relation
to that of the occupied countries. Besides providing laborers
for the Reich, these areas were forced to send most of their
foodstuffs, industrial raw materials, and finished goods to Germany. Specifically this meant bauxite, iron ore, and oil, as well
as rifles, artillery pieces, and tanks for the German war machine.
In addition, as was typical inside the Reich, these regions had
to put up with the confusing and often conflicting administrative
policies of a number of competing German agencies. The military moved in some of its administrative personnel. Various
governmental ministries, the party, and the SS, especially under the guise of providing security, sent in representatives of their
own. At times, the Gau leaders, who already had extensive power
in their own regions, were allowed to expand their jurisdiction
to adjacent areas. The end result was inflation, dislocations,
financial chaos, and corruption on a grand scale throughout
the occupied lands.

Nazi exploitation and cruelty led portions of the indigenous
populations to undertake acts of vengeance against the occupiers, and the Nazis responded in kind. In May 1942, Czech
resisters assassinated the SS zealot, Reinhard Heydrich, who had
become the governor of the Czech protectorate. In retaliation,
the Nazis leveled the village of Lidice, massacred over 200 men
and women, and sent most of the remaining women and children off to concentration camps. In June 1944, at Oradour-sur-
Glane in France, SS soldiers killed more than 600 residents in
retaliation for their supposed complicity in hijacking truckloads
of gold. Acts such as these could only generate hatred toward
the Nazis, and it is quite apparent that their policy of smash-
and-grab toward the occupied territories was self-defeating. Their
alienation of the occupied populace was bound to grow, for their
thinking was based too much on short-term, exploitative goals.
An even larger miscalculation on the part of the Nazis was to
think their war economy, despite prodigious efforts by some of

their people, would be able to match the combined economic might of Great Britain, the Soviet Union, and the United States.

THE HOLOCAUST

Even though the Jews had been subjected to widespread discrimination, degradations, and deprivations before the war, the Nazis instituted even more heinous actions soon after the conflict began. One of these was mobile killing operations. These units, the *SS-Einsatzgruppen*, sometimes called insertion commandos, were first used in Poland in 1939. Although exceedingly brutal, they had not yet engaged in the wholesale murdering of victims. In the spring of 1941, Hitler decided that units similar to the *Einsatzgruppen* were to be dispatched into Soviet territory after the impending invasion had begun. They were to work behind the front lines and move from town to town, killing all Jewish inhabitants on the spot, though others, including local Slavic leaders, might have to be eliminated as well.

Each fully motorized insertion group contained between 600 and 1,000 persons. The lower ranks were made up of Gestapo, police, military-SS, and a number of specialists, such as interpreters and communications experts. Their leaders were carefully selected, primarily from the SD and were usually from middle-class, professional backgrounds. At first, the insertion groups preferred killing by firing-squad, but the psychological impact upon those doing the shooting was so overwhelming that gas vans, that suffocated their human cargo with carbon monoxide, soon began to appear. The vans proved less than satisfactory, since unloading them and disposing of the "remains" was hard and nauseating work, so the shootings continued. It is difficult to get accurate figures on these operations, but it is estimated that they were responsible for the murder of from 1.5 to 2 million people.

Another Nazi institution, concentration camps, had been in existence before the war. The first, at Dachau, outside Munich, opened in 1933, but initially the SA and SS relied mostly on irregular camps, called wild camps, for the keeping of prisoners. These wild camps were located throughout the Reich and included any facility available—local jails, abandoned warehouses, even party offices. Those committed to the wild camps were not primarily Jews but political opponents who were usually held for indefinite periods before being released. By the mid-1930s, more permanent structures were being constructed. These housed, besides political prisoners and Jews, those considered religious opponents (Jehovah's Witnesses), "unfit" races (gypsies), asocials (habitual criminals, sex offenders), and social undesirables (homosexuals, the mentally deranged, and the physically deformed). Each prisoner wore on his or her striped uniform a color-coded triangle—red for political prisoners, black for asocials, pink for homosexuals. Until 1938, the proportion of Jews to non-Jews committed to concentration camps was relatively equal, but after Crystal Night, the proportion of Jews jumped dramatically and continued to rise throughout the war. Eventually the Nazis built nineteen official camps, but there continued to be many outlying camps outside the main facilities.

The supposed primary function of the SS-administered camps was to provide the laborers for the Nazis. The inmates undertook all types of projects, from felling trees to making clothes. Entire industries that relied upon concentration-camp labor began to take shape as early as 1939—stone quarries at Mauthausen, armament works at Buchenwald, a textile factory at Ravensbrück. During the war, I.G. Farben opened synthetic oil and rubber plants at the new Auschwitz camp, and subterranean factories were built at Dora-Mittelbau to serve nearby industries in central Germany. In addition, the SS contracted prisoners to firms, such as Daimler Benz, Krupp, and Farben to be used as slave laborers.

The work in the camps was hard and exhausting and often broke even the most able-bodied of persons. It went on seven days a week; there were no holidays. Punishment was perpetual, the most frequent form being twenty-five lashes with a rawhide whip. In addition, male prisoners who had committed infractions were often forced to stand at camp entrances all day without food. One of the favorite "sports" of the SS guards was to make prisoners throw themselves on the ground, get up, crawl on their elbows or roll, then jump up and down in a squatting position: this often went on until most of the prisoners were no longer able to move. For major offenders, there were penal blocks with isolation cells. Executions were actually rare, though attempted escapees were killed, and many prisoners died as a result of guard brutality and overwork.

Some of the camps also engaged in unusual types of work, the best-known and most hideous of which were the medical experiments. In these cases, Nazi doctors and technicians performed experiments on prisoners to limit the birthrate of unwanted "specimens" and to try to discover ways in which to hasten the propagation of "preferred" races. The methods used ranged from sterilization, a practice already widespread before the war, to inflicting prisoners with incurable diseases in order to observe the results.

While some of the activities at the concentration camps are almost too horrible to describe, those at the extermination camps were even worse. In appearance, these resembled the concentration camps—located in remote areas (many in Poland) with barracks-like structures for the prisoners and separate compounds for the guards and administrators. Their main function, however, was quite different: they were killing centers. Unlike the mobile killing operations, where the killers sought out their victims, at the killing centers, the victims were brought to their murderers. Their names—Chelmno, Belzec, Sobibor, Treblinka, Auschwitz—will forever be associated with what we now call the Holocaust.

Although historians disagree as to when the systematic killing of Jews was set in motion—Hitler never gave a direct order to that effect—most agree that sometime between the spring and late summer of 1941, the operation commenced. Many also agree that the Wannsee Conference, called by Heydrich in January 1942, did not start the process, but brought together leaders to coordinate what had already become the Nazi extermination policy. By the end of 1941 and beginning of 1942, the death camps were in operation.

The killing centers worked for the most part quickly and efficiently. After having been packed into freight cars for days with no provisions or facilities, individuals would step off a train in the morning and be separated into two groups. Those considered fit for work were sent off to labor camps. Those thought to be incapable of sustained, hard work—the elderly, often women, almost always children—were sent immediately to the gas chamber. They were required to undress in changing rooms and then herded into the shower rooms. Once there, special guards closed the doors behind them, and the gassing, from outlets in the ceiling, began. At first, the guards had used carbon monoxide, but it proved too slow, taking up to two hours to kill all the victims, so the SS turned to crystallized prussic acid, know as Zyklon B, which worked faster, killing the whole group in twelve to thirty minutes, as the main chemical agent. After the screaming had stopped, the guards opened the doors, removed the bodies, and prepared the showers for the next victims. By evening, the corpses had been burned, and their clothes (and the hair of the women) packed away for shipment to Germany to help in the war effort. In a sense, the operation resembled an assembly-line method for the killing of human beings.

Though estimates vary, approximately 150,000 people were murdered in gas vans at Chelmno. At the Belzec, Sobibor, and Treblinka death camps, gas chambers accounted for the deaths of around 1.5 million people. Another 2 million were murdered at Auschwitz, making the total at least 3.65 million. In March 1943, Himmler had decided that Belzec, Sobibor, and Treblinka would be closed, since they had fulfilled their function of eliminating most Jews from central Poland, and since Auschwitz was by then considered capable of meeting most of the Nazis' extermination needs. Nevertheless, Jews in Treblinka staged an uprising in August, and another occurred at Sobibor in October. Even though upwards of 600 prisoners escaped, most were recaptured. Only about 125 of the prisoners from the two camps survived the war. The uprisings did speed up those camps' closings, however, which was accomplished by the end of the year. The camps' buildings were then burned to the ground, the areas covered with dirt and planted with ground cover and trees.

Auschwitz was part of the general evacuation west. As the Red Army advanced in late 1944—in November there was also a brief uprising at Auschwitz—it was likely that the Soviets would overrun the eastern camps. The Nazis therefore decided to close them down, including Auschwitz, and approximately 250,000 prisoners were forced to march west hundreds of miles at the height of winter to reach Germany. The 100,000 who made it were put into already overcrowded concentration camps, where they attempted to survive the final months of the war. They account for many of the Jews whom the Allies liberated in April and May 1945. When Soviet troops had captured the Auschwitz complex in January, they found only 2,819 prisoners alive. The Nazis had not accomplished their overall objective, but few Jews were left to recount the horrors they had witnessed and experienced during those terror-filled years at the camps.

Although 6 million Jews had been purposely murdered within a very short time, others, as mentioned earlier, were also caught up in the Nazis' destruction process. Scholars have put the total figure at 11 million, and besides Jews, the numbers include millions of Slavic people who lived in areas taken over by the Germans as well as thousands of the Nazis' political opponents, gypsies, the mentally ill and retarded, and the physically handicapped. They, too, were victims.

The Nazis also carried out two additional actions that were integral parts of their racial policies. One was the euthanasia program. It originated in the spring of 1939, when the parents of a severely handicapped baby petitioned Hitler to have the child legally killed. Hitler not only consented, he further ordered that a secret program be launched to eliminate other mentally and physically "unfit" children from the Reich. The program was soon extended to adults, and an organization labelled T4 opened several institutions to conduct this ghastly undertaking. Eventually the number of T4 institutions reached six, and they found their victims mainly at asylums and hospitals, but also at concentration camps. Initially, the victims were to be shot, but T4 administrators then decided to use carbon monoxide, and later, like their counterparts in the death camps, they instituted the use of Zyklon B. By August 1941, 72,000 of the T4s' "patients" had been liquidated, but public protests, especially from Bishop Galen of Münster, induced Hitler to call a halt to the program. Nonetheless, euthanasia practices became more decentralized and continued underground. The victims were eliminated primarily by starvation or lethal injection, so that, in the end, about 100,000 mentally and physically handicapped people lost their lives.

The SS also undertook a move in the opposite direction—the promotion of "superbly fit" babies. In 1935, it started what was known as the Lebensborn, or fountain of life program. Eventually they established a number of homes inside Germany and throughout occupied Europe. These homes provided places for pregnant wives of SS men or single women who met strict Aryan guidelines and who had been made pregnant by a member of the SS or the German armed forces, to give birth. Once born, the children were given over for adoption by an SS family, or kept by the mother to be brought up by her. Even though accused of running legitimized brothels, the SS looked on the Lebensborn program as an important step toward forming a master race. Another, even more perverse, Lebensborn activity was the kidnapping of "racially valuable" children, upwards of 200,000, from Polish and Soviet parents, who were then raised by desirable German families. After the war, the Lebensborn children were for the most part shunned, though, obviously, through no fault of their own.

The reaction of various elements in the world to the Nazis' racial policies, and more particularly to their extermination policy, is not reassuring. Among the Germans themselves, the Nazis' actions did generally did not evoke a strong reaction. No doubt millions understood what was happening, and millions more surmised what was happening at the (often) far away "work" camps, but they chose not to believe it, lacking concrete and overwhelming evidence. They were understandably more concerned about their own immediate problems—the Allied bombing raids on the home front and their loved ones and friends on the battlefronts—than they were about the suffering of Jews, for whom most Germany felt little sympathy. But their lack of concern and their inaction is still a stinging indictment of what, with few exceptions, the German people failed to do.

The Allied reaction, while not one of complete indifference, was not much better. News of Nazi atrocities had reached them by the beginning of 1942 through neutral Switzerland and Sweden, and the Vatican and the International Red Cross were also indicating what was going on. Still many, including governmental officials, failed to grasp the gravity of the situation. By

1943–44, some realized the hideous nature of what the Nazis were doing, but any possibility of striking a deal by which Jews would be exchanged for German prisoners of war was difficult to complete, and U.S. and British military leaders were reluctant to bomb the camps or to divert their effort from military targets.

Even the reaction of the Jewish community in the West is disconcerting. As early as the end of 1940, a Jewish Agency representative in Geneva was warning about the horrible treatment of Jews, and during 1941, he sent information to Jewish leaders in Britain, Palestine, and the United States. When the systematic killing started at the end of the year, some well-placed Jews were well aware of the Nazi actions, but they registered little formal protest. They seemed too stunned, too unbelieving, to speak out. By the beginning of 1942, they had recovered their equilibrium and were condemning the reports of Nazi atrocities at every opportunity, but even the Jewish leadership, for a time, had failed to respond to the horrors being inflicted on their fellow Jews.

The destruction process itself involved both perpetrators and victims. Who were these perpetrators? Who was directly involved? In a sense, the answer is many—those who signed the deportation orders, those who put the prospective victims on the trains, those who engineered the trains, the firms that manufactured the killing gas, the men who built the camps, the guards who dealt with the prisoners, the special commandos who administered the gas, the persons who extracted the gold from the victims' teeth. No matter where one draws the line of active participation, the machinery of destruction represented a broad cross section of the German people and their East European accomplices. They were not a group of professional killers as is sometimes alleged. Every profession, every type of worker, every social strata was represented in the mechanism. It is difficult to comprehend how these people overcame their scruples. Discipline obviously played a role, as did repetition—one can do anything if one does it often enough and long enough. Further factors were repression and rationalization—one is only following orders, what can one person do? But these explanations are not completely satisfactory, and the true reasons may never be explainable.

As for the victims, the reactions of Jews were conditioned by their centuries of precarious existence. They tried to find ways around their problems—whether in the ghettos or in the camps. At times they resisted—the most famous being the Warsaw Ghetto uprising of October 1943—even, as mentioned, in the death camps themselves. Most often they tried to escape, and at times some even complied. Whatever their reaction, it is indisputable that one of the most heinous acts in the history of the world took place between 1941 and 1945. Among the many negative aspects of the Nazi regime, their treatment of the Jews is their most horrible and enduring legacy.

RESISTANCE

The German resistance movements differed from those in the rest of occupied Europe in one vital respect: most of the German people were loyal to the regime. The Nazis were not an alien force in their midst, they were genuinely popular. To many Germans, Hitler and his movement were not to be resisted but revered. Nevertheless, there were persons in Germany, who, though small in number and diverse in backgrounds, desired to overthrow the regime. The reasons for their disillusionment varied, but often included taking exception to the regime's arbitrary and criminal nature, its dictatorial oppression, its police excesses, its unwarranted unleashing of another war, its ruthless persecution of its political opponents, religious leaders, and especially Jews.

Those who resisted were never a unified movement, and they faced a number of problems. Since most Germans felt positively about the government, resisters could not depend on a mass uprising in which the populace would join them to topple the regime. Rather, they would have to depend on having key persons in key places to take over when the time was right: only then could they explain the criminal nature of the Nazi movement to the public. They also faced the moral dilemma of opposing their government during a period of all-out war. Even if the resisters succeeded, they would immediately be confronted with the charge of treason. And there was the further and extremely difficult problem of assassinating the Führer. Starting a new regime by committing an immoral act against a government that one is trying to show is immoral obviously presented the resisters with a profound dilemma, but ultimately most of the groups decided that they had to eliminate Hitler. They further realized that killing him would not be easy, for not only did Hitler wear a bullet-proof vest and a metal-lined cap, he had his own specially protected cars, used his own private train and airplane, and kept his movements secret until the last possible moment.

An equally important factor was the preventive purge of active or potential anti-Nazis that the state security apparatus practiced from its inception. In the prewar years, preventive arrests and the outlawing of potential opposition groups rid the Nazis of a number of possible resisters. During the war, this practice continued. Along similar lines, the National Socialists' police-state tactics made underground plotting exceedingly hazardous, for no one could be sure whom to trust. An additional difficulty was Allied suspicion. People associated with resistance groups were able to contact Allied officials on numerous occasions, but these officials usually viewed the German plotters with skepticism. The Allies were simply not ready to aid and encourage sincere Germans filled with pious hopes but with nothing tangible to show for their beliefs. From the Allied standpoint, a failed coup attempt with their complicity would do little more than strengthen the government in the eyes of the German people.

The resistance groups that existed consisted of individuals from all walks of life—blue-collar workers, the middle class, professionals, civil servants, aristocrats—but they seldom had contact with one another. Among the greater German populace in general, it is difficult to ascertain how much disillusionment with the Nazis there actually was. Some people obviously escaped into their private spheres, and uninterrupted solidarity continued to exist in homes, working-class neighborhoods, Catholic parishes, and in the countryside. Obviously, peoples' retreat into their own lives still did nothing to undermine the Nazi state. There was also surprisingly little evidence of work slow-downs or sabotage in factories. At times, people feigned illnesses to avoid going to work or threw sand into factory machines or purposely let equipment run down, but their disgust or disenchantment with the government was usually more passive than active.

Still, there were Germans determined to overthrow the regime. Among the Socialist resisters, who had numerous adherents in exile outside as well as inside the country, Julius Leber was probably the best known. He had been a political opponent of the Nazis from the beginning and had been put in several concentration camps between 1933 and 1937. Upon his release, he made a living as a coal dealer in Berlin, but he remained active in the resistance. When some of the resisters decided to form a "shadow government" that would take over after Hitler was overthrown, Leber agreed to be their interior minister. Leber was arrested in early July 1944, sentenced to death after a show trial, and executed in January 1945. He and his fellow socialists never seemed to have regretted what they had done.

The government harassed the Communist groups immediately after the Nazis assumed power. Some Communists left the country, but others stayed on and never ceased in their efforts to undermine the government. Some, such as Harro Schulze-Boysen, helped to set up a spy ring in Berlin known as the Red Orchestra that sent information to the Soviets until the Gestapo penetrated the group and arrested Schulze-Boysen in 1943. Others, such as Anton Saefkow, attempted to forge closer ties with the Socialists until Saefkow was arrested and executed soon thereafter. The Communist presidential candidate in 1932, Ernst Thälmann, was shot at Buchenwald concentration camp in August 1944. It is estimated that the police and the SD arrested around 150,000 Communists, many during the early years of the regime, and that some 25,000 Communists were murdered or died in concentration camps throughout the period of Nazi rule.

Among youth, there was a good deal of resistance to Nazi measures, but active resistance was confined mostly to college students. Siblings Hans and Sophie Scholl headed a student resistance group known as the White Rose movement at the University of Munich. Their main anti-Nazi activity was the printing and distribution of a number of pamphlets critical of the government. They also developed links with student groups

in other cities, such as Hamburg and Berlin, but those in th
Munich group were arrested in April 1943, and five of them
including Hans and Sophie, were sentenced to death and killec

Even in Austria, where loyalty to nazism was wide and dee
among the population, resistance groups sprang up. The mai
one, the Countermovement, was founded in August 1942, an
at one point had as many as 500 members.

More important was a diverse resistance group known was th
Kreisau Circle. Kreisau was the country estate of a young civi
servant and the descendent of a famous military family, Helmut
James Count von Moltke. Moltke and a widening circle of friend
met at Kreisau and in Berlin a number of times between 194
and 1943 to plot the regime's downfall and to plan for a new
conservative government based on principles of Christian mora
ity. Although hesitant at first to use force against the Führer, the
eventually decided that they had no other choice. The Kreisa
Circle included Socialists, trade union leaders, Protestant an
Catholic theologians, aristocrats, and civil servants among it
members. Besides Moltke, one of the most active was Adam vo
Trott zu Solz, a lawyer in the foreign service who used his po
sition to establish numerous contacts with Allied officials outsid
the country. The Gestapo arrested Trott five days after the Jul
20th plot engineered by the military resisters and condemne
him to death, mostly on the grounds of guilt by association
Moltke had already been arrested in January 1944 and thus ha
nothing to do with the July 20th assassination attempt eithe
but the government executed him in January 1945 at the ag
of 37. Trott had been 35.

There were also a number of other individual resisters wh
had contacts with the military and with the members of th
Kreisau Circle but who pursued an independent course. Per
haps the most outspoken of these was Carl Goerdeler, who ha
resigned as mayor of Leipzig in 1937 in protest to anti-Semiti
actions taken by Nazis living there, and who devoted himself t
building up opposition to the government. Other long-tim
opponents were diplomats Ulrich von Hassell and Ernst Baro
von Weizsäcker, and a number of church leaders, includin
Dietrich Bonhoeffer of the Protestant Confessing Church an
Konrad Baron von Preysing, a Catholic bishop from Berlin. On

of the more enigmatic figures was Wilhelm Canaris, the head of military intelligence. Although never directly involved, Canaris's office provided cover for a number of the resisters to pursue their activities. By the time of the July 20th attempt, Hitler had demoted Canaris to a rather lowly military staff job—Himmler had assumed control of military intelligence—but Canaris was too closely linked with the conspirators, so he, too, was arrested and eventually put to death in February 1945.

The resistance within the military was the most active and the most significant: they had the best access to the Führer. They also had some contact with civilian elements and were heavily involved in the actual attempts on Hitler's life. The most important military resister was Colonel Claus Count von Stauffenberg, although military leaders at the highest levels, like General Ludwig Beck, the former army chief of staff, also participated. Von Stauffenberg had received serious wounds in North Africa in April 1943 and had thereafter been posted to a command center in Berlin. From this position he masterminded the ill-fated July 20th bomb attempt to kill Hitler. A few days before, he had written to his wife: "It is now time that something is done. But he who has the courage to do something must do so in the knowledge that he will go down in German history as a traitor. If he does not do it, however, then he will be a traitor to his own conscience."[2]

As early as 1938, a military group hoped to remove the government, but the Munich crisis over the fate of Czechoslovakia intervened, and the resisters, having failed to get the backing of the British, did not take action. Resisters also had contacts with the British in the summer of 1939 and through the papacy to Britain in the winter of 1939–40, but the attack on Norway and Denmark in April 1940 ended any prospect for a coup. The military conspirators were again active in March 1943, when Colonel Henning von Tresckow, on the eastern front, managed to get a package with a bomb in it placed aboard Hitler's personal plane during his return flight to Berlin. The bomb never went off. Also in March, an army officer, Colonel Rudolf Baron

---

2 Quoted in Peter Hoffmann, *German Resistance to Hitler* (Cambridge, Mass., 1988), 135.

Christoph von Gersdorff, was scheduled to lead Hitler through a Berlin exhibition of captured war material. Von Gersdorff was carrying a concealed bomb and had set it to detonate ten minutes after the tour began. But Hitler went through the exhibit in several minutes without stopping to view any of the captured equipment. After Hitler left, Gersdorff quickly found a bathroom and defused the bomb.

At the July 20, 1944, attempt, the bomb had detonated as planned, but in this instance, Stauffenberg had left the barracks room at Hitler's East Prussian headquarters, where the briefing was being held, before the bomb exploded. He heard it go off and assumed that Hitler had been killed in the explosion, but, as mentioned, the Führer was only slightly injured. Von Stauffenberg had already proceeded to call Berlin to set into motion the planned takeover of the government and the military forces, but when officials and officers loyal to Hitler in Berlin found out that the Führer was not dead, the coup attempt quickly collapsed. Von Stauffenberg and those most intimately connected with the plot were shot immediately. Hitler then had the Gestapo round up other resistance leaders as well as any others who were even slightly suspected of implication. By the time the purge was over, about 7,000 people had been arrested, of whom 5,000 were executed. Many of the conspirators were tried at the infamous People's Court, presided over by the Nazi judge Roland Freisler. Freisler's treatment of the defendants was almost beyond belief. He cajoled, badgered, and belittled them without mercy. For instance, he shouted at the Catholic priest, Alfred Delp: "You wretch, you little pip-squeak of a pastor—and someone like you dares to try to kill our beloved Führer. A rat is what you are. You should be stepped upon and squashed."[3] More than anything else, Freisler's words reflect the heinous, vindictive core of the regime.

The carryover of the German resistance movements has remained controversial. The movements had virtually no effect on the course or outcome of the war, although some persons in Germany have insisted that a more favorable Allied response

---

3 Quoted in Ingo Müller, *Hitler's Justice: The Courts of the Third Reich* (Cambridge, Mass., 1991), 141.

to the groups might have led to Hitler's downfall and a shortening of the conflict. Also at issue has been the moral and spiritual impact of the resistance on postwar Germany. No doubt, there were in the movements a number of high-minded, principled individuals who sought a new Germany that would blend together the best qualities of liberalism, conservatism, socialism, and Christianity into a forward-looking state. Yet what many in the movements envisaged was not a democratic state based upon all the people but a traditional state in which the old elite would again be the dominant force in shaping the destiny of the nation. On the other hand, the individuals who became involved had to have firm convictions to work against a ruthless government that had a monopoly of power and enjoyed the support of most persons in the country. With the Gestapo able to penetrate many resistance groups, many members paid the ultimate price for following their consciences. It was truly a test of the courage of many resisters that they were willing to give their lives combating what they considered to be an unmitigated evil in their midst. Their judgment turned out to be correct.

CONTINUITY IN GERMAN HISTORY?

The dilemmas surrounding Germany's resistance movements are related to another divisive issue in German history, that of continuity. The issue is probably easiest to understand as a series of questions: Was Nazi Germany a continuation of previous trends in German history, trends that harkened back to the nineteenth century and earlier? Or was nazism something new and different, a break from the German past? Did nazism continue the separate path (*Sonderweg*) Germany had been pursuing for some time, or did it exhibit modernizing tendencies as well? In a sense, the issue may not seem difficult to resolve, for National Socialism obviously contained both forward-looking and backward-looking elements. For instance, the Nazis took advantage of intrinsic German features, such as the willingness of the bourgeoisie not to exert political power. And the Nazis also possessed modern characteristics, such as their emphasis on industrial growth. However, the question of the continuity or discontinuity of German history is more complex than whether the Third Reich was traditional or modern, for there were vast differences between Nazi theory and practice, between what they said and what they did.

In the area of culture, the National Socialist position appears clear-cut, for the movement seemed opposed to all that was modern and preferred and actually insisted upon traditional, back-to-the-soil, nationalistic, heroic themes. But even in this sector, there were exceptions, such as in the field of architecture. The Nazis planned new and huge monumental buildings, but retained, and, in some instances, continued the functional trends of many buildings of the Weimar period.

In terms of German society, the difference between theory and practice becomes the defining issue in the continuity-discontinuity debate. In theory, the Nazis proclaimed that they were instituting a social revolution in which class distinctions would disappear. In reality, their revolution was incomplete. The old elite was humbled but did not disappear. The professional and middle class provided significant support for the state but did not benefit as much as they expected. The farming community strongly backed the government, but their already declining position in society was not reversed. The industrial workers were to receive numerous benefits—continuing full employment, fair wages, comprehensive welfare, a house or modern apartment, a car—but they ended up serving in the military or enduring long, hard, even forced hours of work with few advances to show for their efforts. Nazi policies toward women, the churches, and youth were never more than partially effective. In short, they never accomplished socially what they contended they would accomplish.

In foreign policy, the Nazis exhibited a good deal in common with their German predecessors. Even though unified in 1871, the Germans had remained dissatisfied with their position in Europe and in the world. Despite subsequent disclaimers, they had entered into World War I with thoughts of expansion, and this desire for additional territory had not abated even after the war and their defeat. In fact, although the National Socialists raised expansionism to a new level, their aggressive stance fit in well with Germany's earlier thinking.

As in foreign affairs, in the economic realm, Nazi continu-
ies with their recent past outweighed the discontinuities. The
ominance of industry over agriculture became more pro-
ounced than ever before. Large-scale industries were favored
ver smaller ones. State and party involvement in the economy
ccelerated, but the Nazis did not replace capitalism, since they
ealized that business and manufacturing interests were essential
o achieving their objective.

Still, their primary objective was not economic but political.
he Nazi goal of an expanded, racial state could only, in their
ew, result from political decisions made by Hitler and his fellow
azi leaders. The political arena was to be an engine for change,
ad through a series of maneuvers, the National Socialists abol-
hed or gained control over the entire system, from state and
ocal governments to political parties and the media. Yet even
i the political realm, threads of continuity existed. The system
ie Nazis developed was based in large part on the Prussian
uthoritarian tradition. The Nazis may have changed, to an
xtent, the structures and the personnel, but they did not dis-
lace authoritarianism.

Thus the Nazi state was neither exclusively a break nor a
ontinuation of Germany's past. Nor was the regime truly mod-
rn or traditional but a curious amalgam of both. Perhaps it was
ot even unique, given the nationalistic paths taken by France
r Great Britain or the United States or even the Soviet Union
. the time. But what made National Socialism distinctive was
s intention of establishing a state based on race that would
xtend across Europe and, ultimately, the rest of the world.

AFTERWORD/

THE THIRD REICH AS HISTORY

After the war, Germany found itself defeated, divided, and devastated. The Germans had actually anticipated defeat, though the propaganda machine had cushioned its impact almost until the end. The cold war division of the nation into East and West Germany was certainly more perplexing than the defeat itself and in many ways was beyond the people's control. Many Germans probably anticipated losing some territory, but forty-five years of division obviously exceeded their expectations. Other aspects of the devastation were even more permanent. The Germans, with Allied help, were able to overcome the physical destruction that their nation suffered relatively quickly, although the pace was slower in East Germany. But the emotional trauma of World War II and the Third Reich left its scars on the people for a long period. The Allies believed that the Nazis' crimes needed to be exposed, and they, as occupiers, instituted numerous denazification statutes to rid the populace of traces of nazism.

The denazification measures were unevenly applied and not overly effective, but the Allies also held a series of trials at Nuremberg to demonstrate to the world what the Nazis had done. At the main trial, Soviet, British, American, and French judges indicted twenty-four of the most famous Nazis who were still left, including Göring, Hess, von Ribbentrop, Sauckel, Frick, and Speer. The Allies sentenced half of them to death (Bormann in absentia), and gave most of the others lesser sentences. They let off three—von Papen, Schacht, and Hans Fritcsche of the Propaganda Ministry—but German courts later sentenced them to periods of imprisonment. Whether the Nuremberg trials had the desired impact on the German people is debatable, since most were more interested in overcoming the devastation and putting their lives back together than in assuming guilt for the

Nazis' crimes. The Allies could, however, feel at least somewhat mollified in their belief that justice was being done.

The movement of Germany into a different phase of its history did not, of course, prevent historians and commentators from examining the recent Nazi past. They began to look at a number of issues, though usually without resolving them. The most immediate questions were, what had gone wrong? And why had Germany succumbed to National Socialism? The possible reasons, as previously discussed, were many and far-ranging, although a combination of Germany's past and its solution for dealing with world tensions at the time were obviously potent factors. By the 1950s and 1960s, other issues started to come to the fore. Was Nazi Germany an aberration from the German norm, or was it a continuation of what had occurred earlier? Was nazism backward- or forward-looking? Traditional or modern? Again, the answers were not clear-cut, but many began to see Nazi Germany as a society that possessed both traditional and modern features, reaction and progress, continuity and change.

Also during the 1960s, the previously discussed intentionalist-functionalist controversy emerged. It revolved around whether nazism had developed primarily as a result of Hitler's will or because of the polycratic system that the Nazis created. Both elements—the intentions of Hitler and the anarchic functioning of the state—seemed to help explain the dynamics of the regime. In the mid-1980s, another controversy, called the historians' dispute, or *Historikerstreit*, broke out among West German historians, some of whom felt there had been an overemphasis on the treatment of Jews at the expense of the problems the Germans faced toward the end of World War II. The quarrel faded into the background with the rush toward unification in 1989–90, although aspects of the dispute still remain. But all of these issues—and there were others—indicate that despite what historians have accomplished, the nature of National Socialism, like all historical happenings, is still subject to changing interpretations as our appreciation of the era changes.

The various historical controversies further make clear that even though National Socialism exhibited numerous inconsistencies, it was not completely inconsistent and actually demonstrated some constant attributes as well. First is that, in spite of the chaotic nature of the regime, out of the multiplicity of ideas and actions there emerged the duality of party and state, and through the process of coordination, party and state fused into a type of unity. Second, much of the Nazi program was consistent. The ideas of racism, expansion, and war set forth in *Mein Kampf* were ever relevant and continued into 1945. Third, throughout its existence, the Third Reich featured a martial, warlike mentality. Even when not at war, it displayed a belligerent posture. And fourth, the Nazis never deviated from their anti-Semitism. Hatred of the Jews was fundamental to the movement, and its leaders believed that in the future they would establish not only an Aryan-based, but just as important, a Jew-free state. Anti-Semitism was a special German attribute of the broader, authoritarian concept of fascism that arose during the twentieth century.

Nazism also fits into the twentieth century in other ways. No matter how distorted, the movement did have a levelling effect. It considered its mass appeal to be the wave of the future, and it based part of its appeal on displacing the old German elite, admittedly with a much worse version but with a new elite nonetheless. National Socialism further epitomized the twentieth century in its irrationalism, its notion that "there is a bit of Hitler in all of us." And the movement is also related to the breakdown of reality and of traditional, absolute values. Society, in the Nazi view, should consist of myths and symbols, not reality and universal concepts, such as absolute truth or justice or morality except as twisted by the regime. In this sense, their emphasis on the unreal and the irrational, though part of the twentieth century, was all the more damaging to the German people. National Socialism has presented Germans with a difficult legacy to overcome.

BIBLIOGRAPHICAL ESSAY

Since works on National Socialism abound, any examination of them is bound to be a partial one. The following discussion is based primarily on books and articles in English, although some books in German are included when an English equivalent does not exist.

Among the general works, the best is Jeremy Noakes and Geoffrey Pridham, eds., *Nazism: A History in Documents and Eyewitness Accounts, 1919–1945*, 2 vols. (New York, 1983–1988). This wonderful combination of narrative and documents covers almost all aspects of the Third Reich in a comprehensive manner. The editors are preparing a third volume on the most significant omission, the German home front during the war. An excellent synthesis, that includes coverage of the Weimar background and foreign and military policies, is Jackson J. Spielvogel, *Hitler and Nazi Germany: A History*, 2nd ed. (Englewood Cliffs, N.J., 1992). Also good is Otis C. Mitchell, *Hitler's Nazi State: The Years of Dictatorial Rule, 1934–1945* (New York, 1988); and Klaus H. Hildebrand, *The Third Reich* (London, 1984); the latter includes a solid historiographic essay. An outstanding critique with a political and legal emphasis is Karl Dietrich Bracher, *The German Dictatorship: The Origins, Structure, and Effects of National Socialism*, 3rd ed. (New York, 1970). Less satisfactory is William L. Shirer, *The Rise and Fall of the Third Reich: A History of Nazi Germany* (New York, 1960). Among the many criticisms of journalist Shirer's book is Klaus P. Epstein, "Shirer's History of Nazi Germany," *Review of Politics*, 23 (Apr. 1961): 230–245. One is better served reading Shirer's memoirs, *Twentieth Century Journey, Vol. II: The Nightmare Years, 1930–1940* (Boston, 1984), or his diary of that period, *Berlin Diary* (New York, 1941).

Also worthwhile are the relevant portions of general histories of modern Germany, including the masterfully written Gordon A. Craig, *Germany, 1866–1945* (Oxford, 1978), and Hajo

Holborn, *History of Modern Germany, Vol. III: 1840–1945* (New York, 1969); Dietrich Orlow, *A History of Modern Germany: 1871 to the Present,* 2nd ed. (Englewood Cliffs, N.J., 1991); and Volker R. Berghahn, *Modern Germany: Society, Economy and Politics in the Twentieth Century,* 2nd ed. (New York, 1987). Collections of documents are Benjamin Sax and Dieter Kuntz, eds., *Inside Hitler's Germany: A Documentary History of Life in the Third Reich* (Lexington, Mass., 1991), and the older but still useful Joachim Remak, ed., *The Nazi Years, A Documentary History* (Englewood Cliffs, N.J., 1969). Eyewitness accounts have been brought together in Johannes Steinhoff, Peter Pechel, and Dennis Showalter, eds., *Voices from the Third Reich: An Oral History* (Washington, D.C., 1989), and a discussion of major themes, written by historians, is Allan Mitchell, ed., *The Nazi Revolution: Hitler's Dictatorship and the German Nation,* 3rd ed. (Lexington, Mass., 1990).

A superior interpretative work is Ian Kershaw, *The Nazi Dictatorship: Problems and Perspectives of Interpretation,* Rev. ed. (Baltimore, 1989). Also helpful are John Hiden and John Farquharson, *Explaining Hitler's Germany: Historians and the Third Reich,* 2nd ed. (London, 1989); and Pierre Ayçoberry, *The Nazi Question: An Essay on the Interpretations of National Socialism, 1922–1975* (New York, 1981). Jeffrey Herf addresses the bringing together of nationalism and technology under nazism in *Reactionary Modernism: Technology, Culture and Politics in Weimar and the Third Reich* (Cambridge, Mass., 1984). A collection of mainly functionalist essays is H. W. Koch, ed. *Aspects of the Third Reich* (London, 1985). See also the pertinent essays in Hans Mommsen, *From Weimar to Auschwitz: Essays in German History* (Princeton, N.J., 1991).

Among the reference works, a recent bibliography is Helen Kehr and Janet Langmaid, comps. *The Nazi Era, 1919–1945: A Select Bibliography of Published Works from the Early Roots to 1980* (London, 1987). Annotated bibliographies of articles published between 1973 and 1982 are *The Third Reich, 1933–1939* (Santa Barbara, Calif., 1984), and *The Third Reich at War: A Historical Bibliography* (Santa Barbara, Calif., 1984). Robert Wistrich's *Who's Who in Nazi Germany* (London, 1982) contains numerous biographical entries. Another excellent reference is Christian Zentner and Friedemann Bedürftig, eds. *The Encyclopedia of the*

Third Reich, 2 vols. (New York, 1991). For the organization of the government and party, there is the old but still useful Otto Neuberger, *Official Publications of Present-Day Germany* (Washington, D.C., 1942).

A good place to start in studying Hitler is by reading his own words. Besides *Mein Kampf* (Boston, 1943) and *Hitler's Secret Book* (New York, 1961), see *Hitler's Table Talk, 1941–1944* (New York, 1953) and François Genoud, ed., *The Testament of Adolf Hitler: The Hitler-Bormann Documents, February-April 1945* (London, 1961). The Führer's speeches have been collected in Max Domarus, ed., *Hitler: Speeches and Proclamations 1932–1945*, 4 vols. (Wauconda, Ill., 1990–1992). The best biography is Joachim Fest, *Hitler*, (London, 1974), but Alan Bullock, *Hitler: A Study in Tyranny* (New York, 1964) is also a standard. In addition, see Bullock's *Hitler and Stalin: Parallel Lives* (London, 1991). One of the earliest biographies is that of a social democratic journalist, Konrad Heiden, *Der Führer: Hitler's Rise to Power* (Boston, 1944). An excellent short treatment is Helmut Heiber, *Adolf Hitler: A Short Biography* (London, 1961). Two of the many psychological studies are Robert G. L. Waite, *The Psychopathic God: Adolf Hitler* (New York, 1977), and Walter C. Langer, *The Mind of Adolf Hitler: The Secret Wartime Report* (New York, 1973). A helpful reference is Milan Hauner, *Hitler: A Chronology of His Life and Times* (London, 1983). Interpretative works include William Carr, *Hitler: A Study in Personality and Politics* (London, 1978); Sebastian Haffner, *The Meaning of Hitler* (London, 1979); and Eberhard Jäckel, *Hitler in History* (Hanover, N.H., 1984). Ian Kershaw's *Hitler* (London, 1991), and *The Hitler Myth: Image and Reality in the Third Reich* (Oxford, 1987), discuss the Führer's use of power and public opinion. Special aspects of Hitler's life and thought are dealt with in Werner Maser, *Hitler's Mein Kampf: An Analysis* (London, 1970); Eberhard Jäckel, *Hitler's Weltanschauung* (Middletown, Conn., 1972); Milan Hauner, "Did Hitler Want a World Dominion?" *Journal of Contemporary History*, 13 (Jan. 1978): 15–32; Michael H. Kater, "Hitler in a Social Context," *Central European History*, 14 (Sept. 1981): 243–272; and Gerhard L. Weinberg, "Hitler's Image of the United States," *American Historical Review* 69 (July 1964): 1006–1021. For his youth, see Bradley L. Smith, *Adolf Hitler: His Family, Childhood and Youth*

(Stanford, 1967); William A. Jenks, *Vienna and the Young Hitler* (New York, 1960); and Franz Jetzinger, *Hitler's Youth* (London, 1958).

Sketches of other Nazi leaders are contained in Ron Smelser and Rainir Zitelmann, eds., *The Nazi Elite: 22 Biographical Sketches* (London, 1993). Among the memoir literature, see Louis Lochner, ed., *The Goebbels Diary [1942–1943]* (New York, 1948); *Final Entries 1945: The Diaries of Joseph Goebbels* (New York, 1978); Hjalmar Schacht, *Confessions of "the Old Wizard"* (Boston, 1956); *idem, My First Seventy-Six Years* (London, 1955); and Hermann Rauschning, *The Voice of Destruction* (New York, 1940), the latter on his conversations, not always recalled accurately, with Hitler in 1932–34. In a category of their own is Albert Speer's memoirs, *Inside the Third Reich* (New York, 1970), and *Spandau: The Secret Diaries* (New York, 1976). Speer was a very perceptive observer of Hitler and of those around him, although he left out some of his own less than honorable conduct during the regime. For negative appraisals, see Geoffrey Barraclough, "What Albert Speer Didn't Say," *New York Review of Books*, 15 (June 7, 1971): 6–15, and Matthias Schmidt, *Albert Speer: The End of a Myth* (New York, 1984). The memories of Otto Wagener contain excellent material on Hitler's economic views during the late 1920s and early 1930s. They are recounted in Henry A. Turner, Jr., ed., *Hitler: Memoirs of a Confidant* (New Haven, Conn., 1985). Among the biographies, the best on Himmler is Richard Breitman, *The Architect of Genocide: Himmler and the Final Solution* (New York, 1991). Less adequate is Peter Padfield, *Himmler: Reichsführer-SS* (London, 1990). For Ley, there is Ronald Smelser, *Robert Ley: Hitler's Labor Leader* (New York, 1988). Well-written, popular biographies by Roger Manvell and Heinrich Fraenkel include *Dr. Goebbels: His Life and Death* (New York, 1960); *Hermann Göring* (London, 1962); and *Himmler* (London, 1965).

In the Nazi run-up toward power, George Mosse studies the ideological background in his *The Crisis of Nazi Ideology* (New York, 1964), and *Nazi Culture* (New York, 1965). Two short, excellent books on the last years of Weimar are A. J. Nichols, *Weimar and the Rise of Hitler,* 3rd ed. (New York, 1991), and Martin Brozat, *Hitler and the Collapse of Weimar Germany* (Leamington Spa, 1987). Four interpretative essays are contained in Ian

Kershaw, ed., *Weimar: Why Did German Democracy Fail?* (London, 1990). Peter D. Stachura discusses Strasser's role in *Gregor Strasser and the Rise of Nazism* (London, 1983). Among the sociological studies of Hitler's early followers, see Theodore Abel's *The Nazi Movement Why Hitler Came to Power* (New York, 1966, c. 1934); Peter Merkl's expanded version of Abel's data, *Political Violence under the Swastika: 581 Early Nazis* (Princeton, N.J., 1975); and Detlev Mühlberger's *Hitler's Followers: Studies in the Sociology of the Nazi Movement* (London, 1991). On voting patterns, there are Thomas Childers, *The Nazi Voter: The Social Foundations of Fascism in Germany, 1919–1933* (Chapel Hill, N.C., 1983), and Richard F. Hamilton, *Who Voted for Hitler?* (Princeton, N.J., 1982). Two excellent regional studies are Jeremy Noakes, *The Nazi Party in Lower Saxony, 1921–1933* (London, 1971), and Geoffrey Pridham, *Hitler's Rise to Power: The Nazi Movement in Bavaria 1923–1933* (London, 1973).

On politics, the outstanding work is Martin Broszat, *The Hitler State: The Foundations and Development of the Internal Structure of the Third Reich* (London, 1981). One of the early classics is Franz L. Neumann, *Behemoth: The Structure and Practice of National Socialism, 1933–1944*, 2nd ed. (New York, 1944). The best treatment of the Nazi takeover remains Karl Dietrich Bracher, Wolfgang Sauer, and Gerhard Schulz, *Die nationalsozialistische Machtergreifung: Studien zur totalitären Herrschaftssysstem in Deutschland 1933–34* (Cologne, 1965). Also well done are the essays in Peter D. Stachura, ed., *The Nazi Machtergreifung* (London, 1983). William Sheridan Allen's *The Nazi Seizure of Power: The Experience of a Single German Town, 1930–1935*, Rev. ed. (Chicago, 1984), recounts what happened in the fictitious town of Thalburg. For events during the period, there are Fritz Tobias, *The Reichstag Fire: Legend and Truth* (London, 1962); Max Gallo, *The Night of the Long Knives* (New York, 1972); and Hamilton T. Burden, *The Nuremberg Party Rallies, 1923–39* (New York, 1967). A detailed, solid account of the civil service, with an emphasis on Frick's Ministry of the Interior, is Jane Caplan, *Government Without Administration: State and Civil Service in Weimar and Nazi Germany* (New York, 1988). For the life of a middle-level bureaucrat, see Hans-Georg von Studnitz, *While Berlin Burns: The Diary of Hans-Georg von Studnitz* (Englewood Cliffs, N.J., 1964). A pathbreaking study on the limitations of the government and party is Edward N. Peterson, *The Limits of Hitler's Power* (Princeton, N.J., 1969). An excellent book on one of the regions is Johnpeter Horst Grill, *The Nazi Movement in Baden, 1920–1945* (Chapel Hill, N.C., 1983).

On the party, the standard work is Dietrich Orlow, *History of the Nazi Party, 1919–1945*, 2 vols. (Pittsburgh, 1969–73). An excellent contribution to social history is Michael H. Kater, *The Nazi Party: A Social Profile of Members and Leaders, 1919–1945* (Cambridge, Mass., 1983). Studies of propaganda include the succinct Z. A. B. Zeman, *Nazi Propaganda*, 2nd ed. (London, 1983); Willi A. Boelcke, comp., *The Secret Conferences of Dr. Goebbels: The Nazi Propaganda War, 1939–43* (New York, 1970); and Ernst K. Bramsted, *Goebbels and National Socialist Propaganda, 1925–1945* (East Lansing, Mich., 1965). The best overall book on the SS remains Helmut Krausnick, et al., *Anatomy of the SS-State* (New York, 1968). Badly dated is Gerald Reitlinger, *The SS: Alibi of a Nation, 1922–1945* (New York, 1957). Specific SS-related topics are dealt with in Robert L. Koehl, *The Black Corps: The Structure and Power Struggle of the Nazi SS* (Madison, Wis., 1983); George C. Browder, *Foundations of the Nazi Police State: The Formation of Sipo and SD* (Lexington, Ky., 1990); and Robert Gellately, *The Gestapo and German Society: Enforcing Racial Policy, 1933–1945* (Oxford, 1990).

On the Nazi system of justice, there are Ingo Müller, *Hitler's Justice: The Events of the Third Reich* (Cambridge, Mass., 1991), and Donald McKale, *The Nazi Party Courts: Hitler's Management of Conflict in His Movement, 1921–1945* (Lawrence, Kans., 1974). Among the many excellent books on the professions, see the relevant portions of Geoffrey Cocks and Konrad Jarausch, eds., *German Professions, 1800–1950* (New York, 1990); and for specific professions, see Konrad Jarausch, *The Unfree Professions: German Lawyers, Teachers and Engineers, 1900–1950* (New York, 1990); Michael Kater, *Doctors under Hitler* (Chapel Hill, N.C., 1989); Geoffrey Cocks, *Psychotherapy in the Third Reich: The Göring Institute* (New York, 1985); and Alan D. Beyerchen, *Scientists under Hitler: Politics and the Physics Community in the Third Reich* (New Haven, Conn., 1977).

On the German military, the best and most inclusive works are *Germany and the Second World War* (New York, 1990 ff.) They are being published as translations of the German semiofficial histories. Among other contributions in English are Matthew Cooper, *The German Army 1933–1945: Its Political and Military Failure* (London, 1978); and the early analysis of Sir John W. Wheeler-Bennett, *The Nemesis of Power: The German Army in Politics, 1918–1945* (London, 1953). A group of essays based on recent scholarship is Wilhelm Deist, ed., *The German Military in the Age of Total War* (Leamington Spa, 1985).

There is no completely adequate book on the Nazi economy, but see Avraham Barkai, *Nazi Economics: Ideology, Theory and Policy* (New York, 1990); Richard J. Overy, *The Nazi Economic Recovery, 1932–1938* (London, 1982); and the comparative study, Alan S. Milward, *War, Economy, and Society, 1939–1945* (Berkeley, 1977). See also the relevant portions of Karl Hardach, *The Political Economy of Germany in the Twentieth Century* (Berkeley, 1980), and Gustav Stolper, Karl Hauser, and Knut Borchardt, *The German Economy: 1870 to the Present*, Rev. ed. (New York, 1967). Two excellent theoretical essays are Charles S. Maier, "The Economies of Fascism and Nazism," in Maier, *In Search of Stability: Explorations in Historical Political Economy* (Cambridge, Mass., 1987), 70–120; and Tim Mason, "The Primacy of Politics—Politics and Economics in National Socialist Germany," in Henry A. Turner, Jr., ed., *Nazism and the Third Reich* (New York, 1972), 175–200. The most important book on economic factors driving the Nazis toward war is Tim Mason, *Arbeiterklasse und Volksgemeinschaft: Dokumente und Materialien zur deutschen Arbeiterpolitik 1936–1939* (Opladen, 1975), but see also his "Labor in the Third Reich, 1933–1939," *Past and Present*, 33 (Apr. 1966): 112–141. A convincing rejoinder is Richard J. Overy, "Germany, 'Domestic Crisis,' and War in 1939," *Past and Present*, 54 (Aug. 1987): 138–168.

On business and industry, Henry A. Turner, Jr.'s *German Big Business and the Rise of Hitler* (New York, 1985) is excellent on the takeover years, and Arthur Schweitzer's *Big Business in the Third Reich* (Bloomington, Ind., 1964) is likewise on the early years of the regime. On individual firms, there are Bernard P.

Bellon, *Mercedes in Peace and War: German Automobile Workers, 1903–1945* (New York, 1990); John Gillingham, *Industry and Politics in the Third Reich: Ruhr Coal, Hitler, and Europe* (New York, 1985); and Peter Hayes, *Industry and Ideology: I.G. Farben in the Nazi Era* (New York, 1987). On agriculture, the best book is Gustavo Corni, *Hitler and the Peasants: Agrarian Policy of the Third Reich, 1930–1939* (New York, 1990), but also helpful is John E. Farquharson, *The Plough and the Swastika: The NSDAP and Agriculture in Germany, 1928–1945* (Beverly Hills, Calif., 1975). Specific economic topics are examined in James D. Shand, "The *Reichsautobahn*: Symbol of the Third Reich," *Journal of Contemporary History*, 19 (Apr. 1984): 189–200; T. E. J. deWitt, "The Economics and Politics of Welfare in the Third Reich," *Central European History*, 11 (Sept. 1978): 156–178; and Anson Rabinbach, "The Aesthetics of Production in the Third Reich," in George Mosse, ed., *International Fascism* (Beverly Hills, Calif., 1979), 189–222. Rabinbach's essay deals with Speer's Beauty of Work bureau.

For the war economy, the most broadly based work is Berenice A. Carroll, *Design for Total War: Arms and Economics in the Third Reich* (The Hague, 1968). Burton H. Klein's *Germany's Economic Preparations for War* (Cambridge, Mass., 1959) and Alan S. Milward's *The German Economy at War* (London, 1965) on the Blitzkrieg "economy" have been supplanted by Richard Overy's "Hitler's War and the German Economy: A Reinterpretation," *Economic History Review*, 35 (May 1982): 272–291. For the story of Hitler's use of gold reserves from Europe's central banks, there is Arthur L. Smith, Jr., *Hitler's Gold: The Story of Nazi War Loot* (Oxford, 1989).

The best book to date on social developments is Detlev Peukert, *Inside Nazi Germany: Conformity, Opposition and Racism in Everyday Life* (New Haven, Conn., 1987), but still of value is David Schoenbaum, *Hitler's Social Revolution: Class and Status in Nazi Germany 1933–1939* (Garden City, N.Y., 1967). Richard Bessel, ed., *Life in the Third Reich* (New York, 1987), contains a group of thoughtful essays on everyday life. An early pathbreaking social analysis is Daniel Lerner, et al., *The Nazi Elite* (Stanford, 1951). Less titillating than its title is Hans Peter Bleuel, *Sex and Society in Nazi Germany* (Philadelphia, 1973). Excellent memoirs with insights into society are Bernt Engelmann, *Inside Hitler's Germany: Daily Life in the Third Reich* (New York, 1986), and Marie Vassiltchikov, *Berlin Diaries, 1940–1945* (London, 1985). On the 1936 Olympics, there are Richard D. Mandell, *The Nazi Olympics* (New York, 1971), and Duff Hart-Davis, *Hitler's Games: The 1936 Olympics* (New York, 1986).

There is no fully adequate volume on Nazi cultural activities, but Peter Adams, *Art in the Third Reich* (New York, 1992), is well illustrated and provides a start. On literature, a survey is Ronald Taylor, *Literature and Society in Germany 1918–1945* (Totawa, N.J., 1980). On drama, see the pertinent portions of H. F. Garten, *Modern German Drama*, 2nd ed. (London, 1964). On architecture, there is Barbara Miller Lane, *Architecture and Politics in Germany, 1918–1945* (Cambridge, Mass., 1968). Painting and sculpture are covered in Berthold Hinz, *Art in the Third Reich* (New York, 1979), and in Henry Grosshans, *Hitler and the Artists* (New York, 1983).

In terms of popular culture, see Jay W. Baird, *To Die for Germany: Heroes in the Nazi Pantheon* (Bloomington, Ind., 1990); Oron J. Hale, *The Captive Press in the Third Reich* (Princeton, N.J., 1964); David S. Hull, *Film in the Third Reich: A Study of the German Cinema, 1933–1945* (Berkeley, 1969); David Welch, *Propaganda and the German Cinema, 1933–1945* (New York, 1983); Michael H. Kater, *Different Drummers: Jazz in the Culture of Nazi Germany* (New York, 1992); and Alan E. Steinweis, "The Professional, Social, and Economic Dimensions of Nazi Cultural Policy: The Case of the Reich Theater Chamber," *German Studies Review*, 13 (Oct. 1990): 441–459. Renata Berg-Pan's *Leni Riefenstahl* (Boston, 1980) is a biography of the famous film director.

The best treatment of education in Nazi Germany is Manfred Heinemann, *Erziehung und Schulung im Dritten Reich* (Stuttgart, 1980). For university education, there are Geoffrey Giles, *Students and National Socialism in Germany* (Princeton, N.J., 1985), and Jacques R. Pauwels, *Women, Nazis and Universities: Female Students in the Third Reich, 1933–1945* (Westport, Conn., 1984). On special schools, see Werner T. Angress's memoir, *Between Fear and Hope: Jewish Youth in the Third Reich* (New York, 1988), and Dennis Shirley, *The Politics of Progressive Education: The Odenwaldschule in Nazi Germany* (Cambridge, Mass., 1992). Gilmer W. Blackburn's *Education in the Third Reich: Race and History in Nazi Text-books* (Albany, 1984), discusses biases in Nazi textbooks, and Hannah Vogt's *A Burden of Guilt: A Short History of Germany, 1914–1945* (New York, 1965), is a translation of a 1950s German text that does not gloss over the negative aspects of the Third Reich.

Excellent on the Hitler Youth is Gerhard Rempel, *Hitler's Children: The Hitler Youth and the SS* (Chapel Hill, N.C., 1989). More broadly conceived is Peter D. Stachura, *The German Youth Movement, 1900–1945: An Interpretative and Documentary History* (New York, 1981). On the carry-over of conditions during World War I, see Peter Loewenberg, "The Psychohistorical Origins of the Nazi Youth Cohort," *American Historical Review*, 76 (Dec. 1971): 1457–1502. Truly riveting memoirs of youth growing up in the Third Reich are Alfons Heck, *A Child of Hitler: Germany in the Days When God Wore a Swastika* (Frederick, Colo., 1985); Horst Krüger, *A Crack in the Wall: Growing Up under Hitler* (New York, 1986); Marianne Mackinnon, *The Naked Years: Growing Up in Nazi Germany* (London, 1987); Melita Maschmann, *Account Rendered: A Dossier on My Former Self* (London, 1965); and Willy Schumann, *Being Present: Growing Up in Hitler's Germany* (Kent, Ohio, 1991).

On women, there is Jill Stephenson, *Women in Nazi Society* (London, 1975), but see also Claudia Koonz, *Mothers in the Fatherland: Women, the Family, and Nazi Politics* (New York, 1987). Additional topics are covered in Leila J. Rupp, *Mobilizing Women for War: German and American Propaganda, 1939–1945* (Princeton, N.J., 1978), and in the relevant portions of Ute Frevert, *Women in German History: From Bourgeois Emancipation to Sexual Liberation* (Oxford, 1989).

There are a number of good monographs on the churches, including John S. Conway, *The Nazi Persecution of the Churches, 1933–1945* (New York, 1969); Ernst C. Helmreich, *The German Churches under Hitler: Background, Struggle, and Epilogue* (Detroit, 1979); and Guenter Lewy, *The Catholic Church and Nazi Germany* (New York, 1964). Paul Ericksen, *Theologians under Hitler: Gerhard Kittel, Paul Althaus, and Emanuel Hirsch* (New Haven, Conn., 1985), examines three prominent theologians who embraced nazism. Klaus Scholder died before completing his authoritative study of the churches, of which only two volumes, *The*

Churches and the Third Reich, 1918–1934 (Philadelphia, 1988), were published.

Books on racism and the Holocaust are almost too numerous to mention. A good bibliography is Abraham J. and Hershel Edelheit, *Bibliography on Holocaust Literature: Supplement* (Boulder, Colo., 1990). Heading a selective list is Raul Hilberg's brilliant *The Destruction of the European Jews*, Rev. ed. (New York, 1985), but see also his insights in *Perpetrators, Victims, Bystanders: The Jewish Catastrophe* (New York, 1992). A good synthesis is George Kren's forthcoming *The Holocaust* (Arlington Heights, Ill.). Other general studies include Lucy Dawidowicz, *The War Against the Jews, 1933–1945*, 2nd ed. (New York, 1986), and Leni Yahil, *The Holocaust: The Fate of European Jewry, 1932–1945* (New York, 1990). An excellent study of public opinion and the Jews is David Bankier, *The Germans and the Final Solution: Public Opinion under Nazism* (Oxford, 1992). Among the many series of essays are Otto Dov Kulka and Paul R. Mendes-Flores, eds., *Judaism and Christianity under the Impact of National Socialism* (Jerusalem, 1987), and Michael D. Ryan, ed., *Human Responses to the Holocaust: Perpetrators and Victims, Bystanders and Resisters* (New York, 1981). Lucy Dawidowicz is critical of some historians in *The Holocaust and the Historians* (Cambridge, Mass., 1981); Michael Marrus takes a more conventional historiographic approach in *The Holocaust in History* (Toronto, 1987). On whether Hitler ordered the Holocaust, see Christopher Browning's *Fateful Months: Essays on the Emergence of the Final Solution* (New York, 1985); *idem, The Final Solution and the German Foreign Office* (New York, 1978); Gerald Fleming, *Hitler and the Final Solution* (Berkeley, 1984); and Sarah Gordon, *Hitler, Germans and the "Jewish Question"* (Princeton, N.J., 1984). Anti-Semitic policies and a lack of systematic planning in the 1930s are highlighted in Karl A. Schleunes, *The Twisted Road to Auschwitz: Nazi Policy toward German Jews, 1933–1939* (Champaign, Ill., 1972). On the SS-Einsatzgruppen, there is Helmut Krausnick and H. H. Wilhelm, *Die Truppe des Weltanschauungskrieges: Die Einsatzgruppen der Sicherheitspolizei und des SD, 1938–1942* (Stuttgart, 1981). A critique of Krausnick's and Wilhelm's study is Alfred Streim, "The Tasks of the SS Einsatzgruppen," *Simon Wiesenthal Center Annual*, 4 (1987): 309–328. A chilling account of one of the insertion squads is Christopher R. Browning, *Ordinary Men: Reserve Police Battalion 101 and the Final Solution in Poland* (New York, 1992). General works on the concentration and death camps include Konnilyn G. Feig, *Hitler's Death Camps: The Sanity of Madness* (New York, 1981), and Yitzhak Arad, *Belzec, Sobibor, Treblinka: The Operation Reinhard Death Camps* (Bloomington, Ind., 1987). An excellent summary is Henry Friedlander, "The Nazi Camps," in Alex Grobman and David Landes, eds., *Genocide: Critical Issues of the Holocaust* (Los Angeles, 1983), 222–231. Among the incredible literature of the survivors, there are Eugen Kogon, *The Theory and Practice of Hell: The German Concentration Camps and the System Behind Them* (London, 1950); Brewster Chamberlin and Marcia Feldman, eds., *The Liberation of the Nazi Concentration Camps 1945: Eyewitness Accounts of the Liberators* (Washington, D.C., 1987); Lawrence L. Langer, *Holocaust Testimonies: The Ruins of Memory* (New Haven, Conn., 1991); Ota Kraus and Erich Kulka, *The Death Camp: Document on Auschwitz* (Oxford, 1966); Alexander Donat, ed., *The Death Camp of Treblinka: A Documentary* (New York, 1979); and Gordon J. Horwitz, *In the Shadow of Death: Living Outside the Gates of Mauthausen* (New York, 1990). Israeli psychologist Dan Bar-on has taken a different approach by interviewing children of Nazi officials forty years later in *Legacy of Silence: Encounters with Children of the Third Reich* (Cambridge, Mass., 1989). Jon Bridgman's *The End of the Holocaust: The Liberation of the Camps* (Portland, Oreg., 1990) follows the harrowing last months of the ordeal.

On euthanasia and genocide, see Benno Müller-Hill, *Murderous Science: Elimination by Scientific Selection of Jews, Gypsies, and Others, Germany, 1933–1945* (New York, 1988); Robert J. Lifton, *The Nazi Doctors: Medical Killing and the Psychology of Genocide* (New York, 1986); and Robert Proctor, *Racial Hygiene: Medicine under the Nazis* (Cambridge, Mass., 1988). On Lebensborn, there is Marc Hillel and Clarissa Henry, *Of Pure Blood* (New York, 1976), and on the treatment of homosexuals, Richard Plant, *The Pink Triangle: The Nazi War Against Homosexuals* (New York, 1986). On the Allied reaction to the Final Solution, or lack of it, see Martin Gilbert, *Auschwitz and the Allies: A Devastating Account of How the Allies Responded to the News of Hitler's Mass Murders* (New York, 1981), and Walter Laqueur, *The Terrible Secret: An Investigation into the Suppression of Information about Hitler's "Final Solution"* (London, 1980).

On Nazi foreign policy in the 1930s, Gerhard L. Weinberg's *The Foreign Policy of Hitler's Germany,* 2 vols. (Chicago, 1970–1980), and Donald Cameron Watt's *How War Came: The Immediate Origins of the Second World War, 1938–1939* (New York, 1989), are comprehensive. Keith Eubank's *The Origins of World War II* (Arlington Heights, Ill., 1990) is an excellent synthesis. Among the many interpretive works, see Klaus Hildebrand, *The Foreign Policy of the Third Reich* (London, 1973).

An outstanding book on the German public response to World War II is Marlis Steinert, *Hitler's War and the Germans: Public Mood and Attitudes during the Second World War* (Athens, Ohio, 1977). The SD reports upon which Steinert's book is based have been brought together in Heinz Boberach, hrsg., *Meldungen aus dem Reich: Die geheimen Lageberichte des Sicherheitsdienstes der SS 1938– 1945,* 17 vols. (Herrshing, 1984). An excellent overall account of Hitler's war aims and Nazi rule of Occupied Europe is Norman Rich, *Hitler's War Aims,* 2 vols., (New York, 1973–74). A synthesis is Earl R. Beck, *The European Home Fronts, 1939–1945* (Arlington Heights, Ill., 1993). For the situation in Upper Austria, see the relevant portions of Evan B. Bukey, *Hitler's Hometown: Linz, Austria, 1908–1945* (Bloomington, Ind., 1986). Foreign labor is discussed in Edward L. Homze, *Foreign Labor in Nazi Germany* (Princeton, N.J., 1967), and more broadly in Ulrich Herbert, *A History of Foreign Labor in Germany, 1880–1980: Seasonal Workers/ Forced Laborers/Guest Workers* (Ann Arbor, Mich., 1990). On German thinking about eastern resettlement, there is Robert L. Koehl, *RKFVD: German Resettlement and Population Policy, 1939– 1945* (Cambridge, Mass., 1957); on Lidice, see Callum A. MacDonald, *The Killing of SS Obergruppenführer Reinhard Heydrich* (New York, 1989); and for Oradour-sur-Glane, Robin Mackness, *Massacre at Oradour* (New York, 1989). The Waffen-SS is well covered in Bernd Wegner, *The Waffen-SS: Organization, Ideology and Function* (Oxford, 1990), and George H. Stein, *The Waffen-SS: Hitler's Elite Guard at War, 1939–1945* (Ithaca, N.Y., 1966). Mark Walker's *German National Security and the Quest for Nuclear Power, 1939–1949* (New York, 1989), discusses nuclear developments in wartime Germany. On Hitler's suicide, the best account is still the reconstruction of Hugh R. Trevor-Roper, *The Last Days of Hitler* (London, 1950), but additional Soviet details are provided in Lev Bezymenski, *The Death of Adolf Hitler: Unknown Documents from Soviet Archives* (New York, 1968). A well-written synthesis is James P. O'Donnell, *The Bunker: The History of the Reich Chancellery Group* (Boston, 1978).

On the German resistance, the best general work is Peter Hoffmann, *The History of the German Resistance, 1933–1945* (Cambridge, Mass., 1977), but see also his *German Resistance to Hitler* (Cambridge, Mass., 1988), and Michael Balfour, *Withstanding Hitler in Germany 1933–45* (London, 1988). An early rendering is Hans Rothfels, *The German Opposition to Hitler* (Hinsdale, Ill., 1948). Essays by historians and other writers include Francis R. Nicosia and Lawrence D. Stokes, eds., *Germans Against Nazism: Noncompliance, Opposition and Resistance in the Third Reich: Essays in Honour of Peter C. Hoffmann* (New York, 1991); David C. Large, ed., *Contending with Hitler: Varieties of German Resistance in the Third Reich* (New York, 1992); and Annedore Leber, *Conscience in Revolt: Sixty-Four Stories of Resistance in Germany, 1933–45* (Westport, Conn., 1957). On the military resistance and the July 20, 1944, assassination attempt, there are Constantine Fitzgibbon, *20 July* (New York, 1956); Roger Manvell and Heinrich Fraenkel, *The Men Who Tried to Kill Hitler* (New York, 1964); and Pierre Galante, *Operation Valkyrie: The German Generals' Plot Against Hitler* (New York, 1981). A biography of the primary July 20 conspirator is Joachim Kramarz, *Stauffenberg: The Life and Death of an Officer, 15th November 1907–20th July 1944* (London, 1967).

On the Kreisau Circle, see Ger van Roon, *German Resistance to Hitler: Count von Moltke and the Kreisau Circle* (London, 1971). Studies of individuals include Roger Manvell and Heinrich Fraenkel, *The Canaris Conspiracy* (New York, 1969); Heinz Höhne, *Canaris* (Garden City, N.Y., 1979); Christopher Sykes, *Tormented Loyalties: The Story of a German Aristocrat Who Defied Hitler [Adam von Trott du Solz]* (New York, 1969); Gregor Schöllgen, *A Conservative Against Hitler: Ulrich von Hassell, Diplomat in Imperial Germany, the Weimar Republic, and the Third Reich, 1881–1944* (New York, 1991); Gerhard Ritter, *The German Resistance: Carl Goerdeler's Struggle Against Tyranny* (New York, 1958); and James Bentley,

Martin Niemoeller: A Biography (London, 1984). Dietrich Bonhoeffer's moving *Letters and Papers from Prison*, 3rd ed. (London, 1967) tells of the thoughts and quiet heroism of one of Germany's most influential contemporary theologians.

For the Communist resistance, the most comprehensive work is Allan Merson, *Communist Resistance in Nazi Germany* (London, 1985), but also helpful are Heinz Höhne, *Codeword Director: The Story of the Red Orchestra* (New York, 1971), and Gilles Perrault, *The Red Orchestra* (New York, 1969). On the White Rose student group, there are Inge Scholl, *The White Rose: Munich 1942–1943* (Middletown, Conn., 1983); Annette E. Dumbach and Jud Newborn, *Shattering the German Night: The Story of the White Rose* (Boston, 1986); and Richard Hanser, *A Noble Treason: The Revolt of Munich Students Against Hitler* (New York, 1979). A different but enlightening view of nazism is Arnold Krammer, *Nazi Prisoners of War in America* (New York, 1979).

In looking at the Third Reich as history, two excellent works on the Nuremberg Trials are Bradley F. Smith, *Reaching Judgment at Nuremberg* (New York, 1977), and Eugene Davidson, *The Trial of the Germans* (New York, 1966), the latter taking a biographical approach. An exceedingly provocative analysis of nazism that calls into question the concept of modernization is Michael Burleigh and Wolfgang Wippermann, *The Racial State: Germany 1933–1945* (Cambridge, Mass., 1991). Two other influential essays are Leonard Krieger, "Nazism: Highway or Byway," *Central European History*, 11 (Mar. 1978): 3–22, and Wolfgang Sauer, "National Socialism: Totalitarianism or Fascism," *American Historical Review*, 73 (Apr. 1967): 404–424.

Two early attempts to place National Socialism in perspective are Friedrich Meinecke, *The German Catastrophe: Reflections and Recollections* (Cambridge, Mass., 1950), and Ludwig Dehio, *Germany and World Politics in the Twentieth Century* (London, 1959). On the relationship between nazism and fascism, see Ernst Nolte's, *Three Faces of Fascism: Action Française, Italian Fascism, National Socialism* (New York, 1966); Klaus Epstein's critique of Nolte's work, "A New Study of Fascism," *World Politics*, 16 (Jan. 1964): 302–321; and Henry A. Turner, Jr., "Fascism and Modernization," *World Politics*, 24 (July 1972): 547–564. Another article on modernization is Ronald Smelser, "How Modern were the Nazis? DAF Social Planning and the Modernization Question," *German Studies Review*, 13 (May 1990): 285–302.

The historians' dispute in West Germany led to the publication of Richard J. Evans, *In Hitler's Shadow: West German Historians and the Attempt to Escape from the Nazi Past* (New York, 1989); Peter Baldwin, ed., *Reworking the Past: Hitler, the Holocaust, and the Historians' Debate* (Boston, 1990); and Charles S. Maier, *The Unmasterable Past: History, Holocaust, and German National Identity* (Cambridge, Mass., 1988). A good summary is Konrad Jarausch, "Removing the Nazi Stain? The Quarrel of the German Historians," *German Studies Review*, 11 (May 1988): 285–301. For a beautifully written, thoughtful analysis of National Socialism in history, see the relevant portions of Fritz Stern, *Dreams and Delusions: The Drama of German History* (New York, 1987).

INDEX

Nazi Germany
Copy editor, Andrew J. Davidson
Production editor, Lucy Herz
Typesetter, Bruce Leckie
Printer, BookCrafters, Inc.
Book designer, Roger Eggers

About the Author: Alan F. Wilt is professor of history at Iowa State University. In addition to having written *Nazi Germany* for our European History Series, he is the author of *The Atlantic Wall: Hitler's Defenses in the West, 1941–1944*; *The French Riviera Campaign of August 1944*; and *War from the Top: German and British Military Decision Making During World War II*; as well as numerous scholarly articles and reviews. Professor Wilt was given the State of Iowa Regents' Faculty Excellence Award for 1993.